UN... ...TINGHAM
W... ...AWN

ROM THE LIBRAR

The Cup
that Cheers

Strengthens
Nerves
and ensures
Restorative Sleep

IT is wonderful what a difference 'Ovaltine' can make to your outlook on life. This delicious food beverage provides the nutritive elements that build up the health and fitness which keep you cheerful and confident. A cupful at bedtime will do much to ensure natural, energy-creating sleep.

'Ovaltine' is scientifically prepared from Nature's best foods. Its special properties—which help to induce sleep and make it so refreshing and nerve-restoring—are due to the high quality of its constituents and exclusive scientific methods of manufacture.

The unique value of 'Ovaltine' as a bedtime and daytime beverage has been proved by thousands of people throughout the world.

Drink
Delicious # Ovaltine
The Restorative Food Beverage

CHILDREN IN BONDAGE

THE SAVE THE CHILDREN FUND POST-WAR COMMITTEE

Mrs. GLADYS SKELTON, *Chairman*

Miss MOSA ANDERSON
Mr. A. E. BACKHOUSE
Mr. HUMPHREY BOWMAN,
 C.M.G., C.B.E.
Lady BARTON, C.B.E.
Mr. JOHN COFFMAN
Mrs. DE BUNSEN

Captain G. F. GRACEY,
 D.S.O.
Miss RHODA HARRIS
Miss K. M. MINTY
Mrs. G. J. PONSONBY
Mr. H. D. WATSON,
 C.I.E., C.B.E.

Joint Secretaries : Mrs. JEANNE MARIE SMALL (*Survey*)
Mr. EDWARD FULLER (*Editorial*)

The costs of making this Survey have been borne, in part, by the Fitton Trust.

CHILDREN IN BONDAGE

A SURVEY OF CHILD LIFE IN THE OCCUPIED COUNTRIES OF EUROPE AND IN FINLAND

CONDUCTED BY
THE SAVE THE CHILDREN FUND

UNIVERSITY COLLEGE LIBRARY
MAY 29 1943
NOTTINGHAM

PUBLISHED FOR THE SAVE THE CHILDREN FUND BY
LONGMANS, GREEN AND CO.
LONDON · NEW YORK · TORONTO
1942

DECEMBER 1942

PUBLISHED FOR THE SAVE THE CHILDREN FUND, INCORPORATED,
20 Gordon Square, London, W.C.1

by

LONGMANS, GREEN AND CO., LTD.,
of Paternoster Row.

43 Albert Drive, London, S.W.19.
17 Chittaranjan Avenue, Calcutta.
Nicol Road, Bombay.
36a Mount Road, Madras.

LONGMANS, GREEN AND CO.
55 Fifth Avenue, New York.
221 East 20th Street, Chicago.

LONGMANS, GREEN AND CO., LTD.,
215 Victoria Street, Toronto.

BOOK
PRODUCTION
WAR ECONOMY
STANDARD

This book is produced in conformity
with the authorised economy standards

Made in Great Britain

Printed and bound by the LONDON CALEDONIAN PRESS LTD.,
74 Swinton Street, Gray's Inn Road, London, W.C.1.

CONTENTS

PAGE

FOREWORD 7

THE DECLARATION OF THE RIGHTS OF THE CHILD
(DECLARATION OF GENEVA) 10

BELGIUM 11

CZECHOSLOVAKIA 19

DENMARK.. 26

FRANCE 32

GREECE 49

LUXEMBURG 59

THE NETHERLANDS 67

NORWAY 75

POLAND 85

YUGOSLAVIA 108

FINLAND 114

APPENDIX:

NOTE ON RATIONING 122

TABLES OF WEEKLY RATIONS 123

COMPARATIVE TABLES OF RATIONS 134

Freedom from Fear
Freedom from Want

THE SAVE THE CHILDREN FUND
by its international work of relief and
social recovery seeks to apply the principles
of the Atlantic Charter to

EVERY CHILD'S LIFE

These principles were anticipated by the
Founder's Declaration of Geneva (see page 10)
which claims for every child the means requisite for normal development, without
distinction of race, nationality or creed.
Bequests and New Subscribers are specially
needed to maintain the work of Saving the
Rising Generation at Home and Abroad.

THE SAVE THE CHILDREN FUND

President : The Rt. Hon. Lord Noel-Buxton, P.C.
Chairman and Hon. Treasurer : Mr. H. D. Watson,
    C.I.E., C.B.E.
Vice-Chairman : Mr. A. E. Backhouse.
Hon. Auditor : The Lord Plender, C.B.E.
General Secretary : Captain G. F. Gracey, D.S.O.

20 GORDON SQUARE, LONDON, W.C.1

FOREWORD

The general public cannot but be aware of the hardships and privations endured by all people living in the Occupied Countries of Europe, but even now the extent of their sufferings is fully known, perhaps, only to a few. No single aspect of their lives, economic, social or domestic, is unaffected, and the lot of the children in these countries must arouse universal pity and concern.

The Save the Children Fund was founded in England after the last war to bring relief to the suffering children of Europe. Since then, the movement has assumed world-wide proportions as an instrument for promoting child welfare and for raising the standards of child protection, and the national organisations of twenty-seven countries are linked together in an international body at Geneva, the Save the Children International Union.

In common with other of the voluntary organisations which have international affiliations, the Save the Children Fund has set up a special Committee to consider the problems of Post-War Reconstruction in Europe. His Majesty's Government has requested these organisations to prepare and submit plans of work which they are competent and willing to undertake, in order that the British and Allied Governments may use their machinery, personnel and experience to assist in the administration of relief and in the formidable task of reconstructing the social services of the Occupied Countries.

The following report on conditions in the Occupied Countries of Europe has been prepared for the Post-War Committee of the Save the Children Fund. The Fund is primarily concerned with the present and future needs of children, but in this survey it has been felt necessary to give very briefly some account of the background of the children's lives, the economic conditions of the country, the situation as regards food, clothing, and other necessities, as well as the movements of population, with their effects on family life.

Though the survey of each country follows the general plan given above, conditions vary very greatly in the Occupied Countries. In some, as in Poland and parts of Yugoslavia, the civil life of the people has been totally disrupted, the machinery of the social services has been destroyed altogether by the occupying Power, or so hampered by the elimination of trained personnel, by mass deportations and by lack of money that it can no longer work. In other countries, such as Holland, Belgium and Norway, the machinery still exists and still functions courageously, in spite of heavy handicaps. In each survey, therefore, a note has been added of the present conditions of social and welfare services, whether State or voluntary.

The information embodied in this report has been given by certain of the Allied Governments now in Great Britain, to all of whom the Save the Children Fund wishes to express its deep sense of gratitude. Officials of many of the Allied Governments have checked and collated the data received from other sources and, in view of their many and grave preoccupations, their help in this respect is a debt which we cannot hope to discharge but gladly acknowledge. Our thanks are also due to the Ministry of Information for the access freely given to their records. Further, we wish to acknowledge our great obligation to the Save the Children International Union at Geneva for various reports from Occupied Countries which we have received from them. It is on information supplied from this source that the report on Finland is based and, though Finland is not properly an Occupied Country, the material was thought so valuable, in showing what war means in the lives of children, that we have included it in this survey. With the exception of Finland, which is placed as an addendum, the countries are given in alphabetical order.

The ground plan of the survey was drawn up by the joint secretaries of the Post-War Committee, Mrs. Jeanne Marie Small and Mr. Edward Fuller (Editorial Secretary of the Fund). It is, however, Mrs. Small who has borne the chief burden of preparing this report, a task for which she was well fitted by her past experience, as Secretary-

General of the Save the Children International Union at Geneva and by her long and intimate acquaintance with the problems of child-life throughout the world. None the less, the work has been long and arduous and the Committee wishes to place on record its deep appreciation of her devotion and ability.

Terrible as are the conditions revealed by the bare facts given in this survey, the Save the Children Fund is convinced that they must become yet more dire as the war continues and the resources of each country are further depleted by the ruthless exploitation of the German Government. The survey incorporates information which was available up to June 1942. It may become out of date, even before it is published, but unhappily only by an exacerbation of the deprivations and sufferings here shown to exist in a degree which has probably never been surpassed, and seldom paralleled, on the long Via Dolorosa of the human race.

GLADYS SKELTON,

Chairman,
Post-War Committee.

The Save the Children Fund,
20 Gordon Square,
London, W.C.1.
November 1942.

The Declaration of Geneva

By the present Declaration of the Rights of the Child, commonly known as the ' Declaration of Geneva ', men and women of all nations, recognising that Mankind owes to the Child the best that it has to give, declare and accept it as their duty that, beyond and above all considerations of race, nationality or creed :

I.   THE CHILD must be given the means requisite for its normal development, both materially and spiritually.

II.   THE CHILD that is hungry must be fed ; the child that is sick must be nursed ; the child that is backward must be helped ; the delinquent child must be reclaimed ; and the orphan and the waif must be sheltered and succoured.

III.   THE CHILD must be the first to receive relief in times of distress.

IV.   THE CHILD must be put in a position to earn a livelihood and must be protected against every form of exploitation.

V.   THE CHILD must be brought up in the consciousness that its talents must be devoted to the service of its fellowmen.

Drafted by Eglantyne Jebb, founder of the Save the Children Fund, 1922.   Adopted by the General Council of the Save the Children International Union, February 1923. Adopted by the Assembly of the League of Nations, 1924, and reaffirmed 1934.   Signed by the Prime Minister of Great Britain and the Dominion Prime Ministers, 1931.

CHILDREN IN BONDAGE

A Survey of Child Life in the Occupied Countries of Europe and in Finland.

BELGIUM *

I. GENERAL CONDITIONS

Though an occupied country, Belgium has retained most of its pre-war system of administration, which functions, however, under the close supervision of the occupying Authorities.

In 1938, Belgium had 8,304,600 inhabitants, of whom 1,840,600 or 22·1 per cent. were under 15 years of age.

Present Economic Conditions

Belgium is a highly industrialised country, only one-sixth of the population being engaged in agriculture. In consequence, over half the caloric value of the total food requirements had to be imported and, if feeding stuffs for beef and dairy cattle be reckoned as well, the total imports necessary were over 70 per cent.

The catastrophic effect of the all-but-total cessation of imports since the occupation on a country thus circumstanced can well be imagined. The one exception is the import of wheat and other cereals from Germany, which has maintained the bread ration at 225 grammes per day, though arrangements made with Russia for the import of wheat never came into force, owing to Russia becoming involved in the war.

Agriculture.—Because of the shortage of fodder, cattle have had to be slaughtered and a certain proportion of the meat, either fresh or tinned, was requisitioned or bought by Germany. The home production of potatoes used to be adequate for all needs, but as part of the potato crop is used for feeding livestock and part for mixing with cereals to make bread, a much smaller quantity of potatoes is now available for direct domestic consumption.

In 1940 all crops were below the average, partly in consequence of the fighting, partly owing to exceptional weather conditions.

---

* Most of the information concerning food and health is taken from reports prepared by Professor E. J. Bigwood for the Belgian Commission for the Study of Post-War Problems and dated July 30, 1941, and February 1942.

11

Industry.—Belgian industry has been slowed down by lack of certain raw materials ; in consequence there is a great deal of unemployment. Workers may be forced by Labour Exchanges to work in France or Germany, if they do not volunteer to do so, under the threat of having unemployment benefit discontinued. There are about 200,000 Belgians now working in Germany and 100,000 were reported to be working in France in September, 1941, mainly on the coast, for the repair of ports.

Wages have been raised, but not in proportion to the cost of living.

Movements of Population

How many people fled from their homes when the country was invaded is not exactly known. It is estimated, however, that the number amounted to about a million and a half. These refugees fall into two groups : those who were overtaken by the advancing German armies, either in Belgium itself or in Northern France, and those who reached the then uninvaded portion. Some 650,000 Belgians were in the unoccupied zone when the armistice was signed. Those of the first group, who had not gone very far from their homes, returned by their own means within a few days ; others of the first group and the whole of the second group, amounting to 1,200,000 persons, were repatriated either by road or rail between July 1st and the end of September, 1940. This was a stupendous task in view of the disorganisation of transport in France, and the difficulty of provisioning the trains or the rest centres which had been set up every 40 kilometres along the main roads.*

It must be remembered, too, that about 20,000 Belgians, mostly fishermen or people living on or near the coast, tried to escape to France by sea but had to land in Britain, where they are now assisted by their own Government.

Food

Since the end of 1940, there has been very little change in the scale of rations published each month, but the proportion of supplies which are really available has been

---

* See *Croix-Rouge de Belgique*, May–December 1940,

steadily decreasing. It is said that the scale has not been adjusted for fear of the depressing effect it would have on the population.

The daily bread ration of 225 grammes (pre-war average consumption 430 grammes) is generally available, but the fat ration in particular is not, and the potato ration, which in theory is almost equal to pre-war consumption (500 grammes per day), is in fact not more than 30 to 100 grammes per day in towns.

It was estimated that during the first half of 1941 rationing covered only 40 per cent. of the normal needs of adults and 40 to 50 per cent. of the needs of pregnant and nursing mothers (including the increased milk allowance). There is as yet little caloric deficiency in the diet of children under 4, but the deficiency is more marked at every increase of age. This deficiency, for example, is about 20 per cent. for children aged 4 to 6, 20 to 50 per cent. for children of 6 to 14, and over 60 per cent. for young persons.

The situation in the country is slightly better than in urban areas. In the latter, Professor Bigwood calculates that, although the food ration provides theoretically for 1,300 calories (1,400 if available unrationed foods were added), yet, since it is impossible to buy all those foods to which one is entitled, the diet does not in fact amount to more than 900 calories, as against a normal average of 2,500 before the war. Half of these 900 calories are provided by the daily bread ration of 225 grammes.

If the food is considered, not from the caloric but from the body-building point of view, the situation is even more serious in the case of young people :

| | DEFICIENCY IN PERCENTAGES OF NORMAL | | |
	Protein per cent.	Fat per cent.	Calcium per cent.
Pregnant and nursing mothers	60	60 or more	normal
Children 0 to 3 years	normal	10	normal
,, 3 to 6 ,,	normal	50 to 65	40 to 50
,, 6 to 14 ,,	30 to 50 or more	80	50 or more
Young people . .	60 or more	90	80 to 90 or more
Adults	about 60	about 90	65 or more

Those are the conditions for the vast majority of the population, a very small percentage only having either the means or the opportunity to buy in the black market. A study made by Dr. Sillevaerts, in Forest, a suburb of Brussels, among 229 families belonging to three income-groups shows that, whilst from September 1940, to April 1941, the theoretical diet (according to official rations) decreased from 1,500 to 1,350 calories, the actual diet decreased in the higher-income families from 2,700–3,000 to 1,500–1,700, in the medium-income group from 2,000–2,200 to 1,000, and in the lower-income group from 1,500 to 900.

Even during the first three months of 1941, about 60 per cent. of the school children had no breakfast—or no adequate one—a third had an insufficient mid-day meal, and more than half an inadequate evening meal.

For table of rationed foods see Appendix.

Clothing

All textile production is greatly handicapped by the lack of raw materials. In the first half of 1940, raw materials for these industries were available only in the proportion of 33·4 per cent. of the amount for the corresponding period of 1938. Prices are also high : 2,000 francs for an overcoat or a suit, 150 francs for a shirt. In the case of boots and shoes also, the situation is deteriorating.

Soap

Not only is the quantity available insufficient, but the quality is deteriorating. The increase in skin diseases is attributed in part to this cause.

Fuel

In September 1941, the ration was 150 kilogrammes (about 3 cwt.) per month for families up to four persons and 200 kilogrammes (about 4 cwt.) for families of over four persons. Owing to general undernourishment people suffered doubly from the inadequate and often belated fuel supply during the winter of 1941-42.

II. EFFECTS OF WAR CONDITIONS
ON CHILDREN

Nutrition, Health and Growth

In view of the food situation, it is not surprising that the health of children is already seriously affected.

According to reports from the Œuvre Nationale de l'Enfance (the national child welfare organisation responsible for child welfare centres throughout the country), young children are far less robust than formerly ; the proportion of deaths from broncho-pneumonia has increased ; scurvy and rickets, which were extremely rare before the war, are now more frequent, as are anæmia and skin troubles. Among the 350 babies attending an infant welfare centre, 15 died during the first three months of 1941, whereas four to five was the pre-war average. Of these 15, seven were breastfed. Growth is handicapped in about 56 per cent. to 78 per cent. of the children between three and six years of age and in about 51 per cent. to 84 per cent. of those aged six to fourteen.

In an inquiry made in schools during February and April 1941, Professor Jacquemyns established the fact that the proportions of children in poor general health at that date and in May 1940 were as follows :

	May 1940	*January* 1941
Nursery Schools ..	33 per cent.	47 per cent.
Elementary Schools	48 per cent.	63 per cent.
Denominational Schools	20 per cent.	42 per cent.

As regards adolescents, the conditions are worse ; they frequently lose five to six kilogrammes in a four months' period, whilst they continue to grow in height. The same informants report that in the second half of 1941 conditions deteriorated further.

Diseases

There is already a striking increase in tuberculosis. According to the Œuvre Nationale Contre la Tuberculose, the increase is about 100 per cent. At the University Hospital for Children in Ghent, about 3·74 per cent. of the new out-patients in the first four months of 1940 were suffering from tuberculosis ; in the corresponding

period of 1941, the ratio was 7 per cent.   The new clinical
form of pulmonary tuberculosis is acute rather than
chronic and chiefly affects adolescents.   It is very serious
from its onset.

According to reports covering the second half of the
year 1941, scurvy, rickets, skin diseases, anæmia and
eye troubles have increased.   Cases of starvation-œdema
are frequent—three to four cases a week in the out-
patients' departments of the hospitals.

Vital Statistics

We have no precise information, but the child welfare
clinics report that infant mortality is on the increase.

Dr. Schockaert, Professor of Obstetrics at Louvain,
said that premature births due to mal- and under-
nutrition had increased by 300 per cent. in the first half
of 1941.

Education

The use of the Flemish language in schools is encouraged and all Flemish children in Brussels have had to
be transferred to newly created Flemish schools.   This has
met, however, with a certain opposition from the parents,
as many of these children knew French as well as, or even
better than, they did Flemish.

The age limit for teachers—as of other officials—has
been lowered from 65 to 60.   It is hoped that this will
relieve unemployment, since many more teachers were
trained during the past years than there were vacancies
to be filled.   New teachers in communal schools are to be
appointed now by the Ministry of the Interior, assisted
by a temporary advisory commission composed of a
bi-lingual chairman, five Walloon and five Flemish
members.   All teachers' organisations have been amalga-
mated into one corporation, affiliated to the Union des
Travailleurs manuels et intellectuels.

Behaviour and Social Adjustment

There are many indications that the morale of young
people is low ; they are said to think of ' nothing but
jazz and their own enjoyment', in spite of, or perhaps
because of, ' all that is happening around them '.

The number of juvenile delinquents for 1940 was much higher than for the previous years and it is expected that when the 1941 numbers are known they will show a marked further increase.

The number of minors brought to the notice of the Children's Courts by Public Prosecutors and Examining Judges were :

1930	1935	1938	1939	1940
2,526	2,724	2,976	2,942	3,799

The increase is mainly in cases of theft (1,190 cases in 1940 against 667 in 1939), of begging, sexual offences, and truancy. ' The causes are to be found in the disintegration and demoralisation brought about by any social cataclysm, but above all in the deprivations which are the lot of a large section of the population. It is mainly food that is stolen and it is also in order to obtain food that certain children play truant and beg. Sometimes the parents send them round for days on end to beg from farm to farm in the country.'*

Until now no special measures have been taken in the field of juvenile delinquency, and circumstances make still more difficult the task of the children's judges and their assistants, since they can have little influence on the real causes of misconduct. In addition to this, reformatories and similar institutions have such serious catering difficulties that the number of delinquents sent to them must be reduced to the minimum.

Recreation and Youth Organisations

The unification of the various Flemish National-Socialist youth organisations into the National Socialistische Jeugd Vlaanderen was proclaimed. The latter comprises boys' and girls' groups, and aims at working in collaboration with the Hitler Youth.

III. AMELIORATIVE MEASURES*
Activity of Pre-War Services

Welfare, health and educational services, whether official, semi-official or private, continue to work very

---

* See ' Les Répercussions sociales des circonstances actuelles sur l'enfance ' (1940–1941), by Aimée Racine, *Bulletin de l'Union internationale de Secours aux Enfants et Revue internationale de l'Enfant*, Geneva, 1942, Vol. VI, No. 1–5.   † *Id.*

much on the same lines as formerly, even though the prevailing conditions affect their efficiency.

The Œuvre Nationale de l'Enfance has greatly increased its activity. Before the outbreak of war there were still about a thousand communes without child welfare centres or health visitor services. These are increasing so fast that soon, it is hoped, no single commune in Belgium will be without at least one of these institutions.

New Measures and Relief

The Œuvre Nationale opened recently a ' lactarium ', *i.e.*, a centre where women's milk is collected and distributed to specially delicate babies.

Following a Decree of May 29, 1941, on the encouragement of breast-feeding, the Œuvre Nationale has organised widespread propaganda, in collaboration with the Ministry of Public Health and the Belgian Red Cross.

Holiday camps organised by the Œuvre Nationale, Pro Juventute, some municipalities, and various other bodies were opened as usual in the summer of 1941. Many new ones, indeed, were started by big industrial and commercial concerns for the children of members of their staffs, to try to alleviate the distress. This example has been followed by private people. Municipalities and a few private schools organised ' day camps ' near the cities, the children being brought there in the morning, spending the day in the open air, and being given at least one good meal before being sent home at night.

The Aide Paysanne aux Enfants des Villes was founded early in 1941 by the National Agricultural Corporation. According to a Decree of June 7, 1941, it exercises a kind of monopoly in billeting town children in the country. It aims at billeting at least 10,000 children, but according to the *Nieuwe Rotterdamsche Courant* of February 11, 1942, it had billeted only about 600 children up to that date. The actual organisation and supervision of the billeting is in the care of the Œuvre Nationale de l'Enfance.

Groups of children were invited to recuperate in Germany, and nearly 2,500 went to Switzerland during the summer of 1941. During the last two winters a relief organisation, the Winter Aid, organised a distribution of

meals and of additional food to school and pre school
children and to pregnant and nursing mothers.

As the needs of the young person seem to be at least
as great as, if not greater than, those of the younger
children, the Winter Aid has, since June 1941, extended
its help to pupils in the middle and technical schools as
well as in the training colleges, and to young people
under 18 who are not attending any school. For this
same age-group, the Red Cross founded a Youth Relief
Committee which provides additional food.

Several thousand tons of foodstuffs (tinned milk and
milk foods, dried vegetables and pulses) have been sent
to the Belgian Red Cross by the International Red
Cross and used in canteens, soup kitchens, etc. The
International Red Cross sent also more than 500,000
Swiss francs' worth of vitamins C and D, as well as
various medicines.

Other new measures for the protection of children
include compulsory vaccination against smallpox between
the third and eighth months of life. In quite another
field, a Decree of March 31, 1941, authorised the Courts
to legitimise children whose parents have been prevented
from marrying by the death of one of them as a result
of the war.

CZECHOSLOVAKIA*
I. GENERAL CONDITIONS

Czechoslovakia differs from most other occupied
countries in that its territory has been dismembered and
occupied by foreign powers in successive stages. We
must therefore distinguish between :

1. Territories incorporated in the Reich :
   (a) The Sudeten territory, according to the
       Munich Award, September 1938,
   (b) The Teschen territory, occupied in October
       1938, by Poland, and in September 1939, by
       Germany.

---

* Most of the information included in this chapter has been
kindly supplied by the Czechoslovak Ministry of Economic Reconstruction, the Czechoslovak Research Institute and the Czechoslovak Ministry of the Interior.

2. The Protectorate of Bohemia and Moravia.
3. The Slovakian Republic.
4. The territories incorporated in Hungary (the whole province of Ruthenia and parts of Slovakia).

Conditions vary from territory to territory, and 1937 must be considered as the last normal year of free Czechoslovakia. Unless otherwise specified, most of the following pages deal with conditions in the Protectorate of Bohemia and Moravia.

Population

The total population of Czechoslovakia was estimated in December 1935 to be 15,159,000 of whom 4,131,000 or 27·2 per cent. were children under 15.

It is estimated that about 3,650,000 former Czechoslovak citizens now live in the territories incorporated in the Reich; 1,500,000 in those incorporated into Hungary; 2,700,000 in Slovakia; and over 7,000,000 remain in the Protectorate.

Economic Conditions

Exact information about the present economic situation is difficult to obtain but, in general, it can be said that the whole economy of the territories incorporated in the Reich and of the Protectorate is governed by Germany's needs. In the Protectorate, the great armament, chemical and other industries are working for Germany. The Sudeten territory produced mainly consumption goods; these industries are much reduced and large numbers of workers are forced to go to work in the Reich. It is therefore probable that there is no unemployment in the different parts of Czechoslovakia.

Slovakia and the territories incorporated in Hungary are mainly agricultural; but the small industries of Slovakia have also to work for Germany and to send there the required number of workmen.

Movements of Population

There has always been a considerable amount of emigration from Czechoslovakia. Before the world economic crisis, between 25,000 and 30,000 people left the country yearly to find employment abroad; then the crisis reduced immigration possibilities, so that between

1932 and 1935 only an average of 5,000 people left each year for other European countries and overseas, rising to about 7,000 in 1936. These people came mostly from the eastern part of the country : Ruthenia and Slovakia. Since 1938, emigration has been limited to those wishing to leave the country for political or racial reasons.

Since the war, many thousands of workers have been shifted more or less compulsorily. No exact figures are available of those Czechs and Slovaks sent to forced labour in Germany after March 15, 1939 ; it can be assumed, however, that the Protectorate has to furnish permanently between 120,000 to 150,000 workers.

Whilst this emigration has a temporary character in the Protectorate, the workers being exchanged after a certain time, conditions are somewhat different in the Sudeten territory, where the Germans admit a loss of population of 8·3 per cent. as a result of emigration. Besides this, large groups of workers and even of women have been sent to northern Germany, Yugoslavia and the occupied parts of the U.S.S.R. under the Labour Service scheme.

Special mention must be made of the Jews, of whom about 90,000 lived in the Protectorate. A few thousands managed to escape abroad and many were deported to Poland, or were interned in the Czech town of Terezin, whose Czech and German inhabitants were told they would be resettled at State expense in a new place of residence of their choice. Of the Jewish population in Slovakia, estimated at 95,000, the local Minister of the Interior announced in the summer recently that 32,000 had been expelled and that not one would be left after September 1942. 144,000 Jews lived before the war in the territories now incorporated into Hungary. According to German sources, 30 per cent. have since been expelled.

There are no figures available about the Jews in those parts incorporated in the Reich, but it is known that a great many of them migrated into the Protectorate. German racial legislation is applied not only in the territories actually incorporated in the Reich but also in the Protectorate.

Food

Conditions vary in the different regions and rationing is much less severe in Slovakia and the territories annexed by Hungary than in other areas.

Czechoslovakia used to be self-supporting for a large number of foodstuffs and had also by 1939 accumulated an important wheat reserve. Soon after the occupation, these stocks were removed to Germany and individual German soldiers and civilians bought and sent home large quantities of food and other goods.

The basic rations in the territories incorporated in the Reich are the same as in the Protectorate, but both in the Sudeten territory and in the Protectorate, Jews have no right to receive fruit of any kind, jam, cheese, fish, poultry, etc., even as a gift.

In Slovakia and the territories incorporated in Hungary, less foodstuffs are rationed and the quantity of the rationed foods is the same as in the Protectorate, or larger.

For the table of rationed foods see Appendix.

Clothing

The number of points required for each article is the same as in Germany but the total number of points in the card is 113 a year instead of 120 as in Germany. Seven points are required for 100 grammes ($3\frac{1}{2}$ oz.) of knitting wool, 20 for a shirt, 120 for a coat, seven for a pair of gloves, etc.

A collection of warm clothing for the army on the Eastern front was made in the Protectorate and over three million articles were obtained, including 69,000 furs and fur jackets, 32,000 blankets and 217,000 sweaters. (*Transocean News Service*, February 8, 1942.)

Soap

The weekly ration is :

   17 grammes ($\frac{2}{3}$ oz.) of refined soap and 83 grammes (3 oz.) soap flakes for babies.

   17 grammes ordinary soap and 83 grammes soap flakes for children two to eight.

33 grammes (1 oz.) ordinary soap and 41 grammes
(1½ oz.) soap powder for anybody over eight.
Soap is not rationed in Slovakia or in Hungary.

Fuel

Fuel is in rather short supply. In Prague, for instance,
1,199 kilogrammes of coal are allowed per head per
year—made up of 824 brown coal (16½ cwt.), 154 kilogrammes of coal (3 cwt.) and 221 (4½ cwt.) of coke. It
is not possible to get more than 50 kilogrammes at a
time except with a special licence. Gas is cut off between
2 p.m. and 6 p.m.

II. EFFECTS OF WAR CONDITIONS ON CHILDREN

Health

No figures are available.

Diseases

Very little is known ; the increased number of deaths
in the Sudeten territory seems to be due mainly to old
age, and to diseases of the heart and cancer, which scarcely
affect children. Tuberculosis, however, is on the increase
and this is a disease most prevalent among the young.

The number of tuberculosis cases (in- and out-patients)
treated at the Bulovka Hospital in Prague is significant :

1937	..	..	.. 10,429
1940	..	..	.. 15,628
1941	..	..	.. 20,396
First quarter of 1942	..		5,255

Vital Statistics

The birth rate has enormously increased in the Sudeten
territory, as it did in Austria and Dantzig after the
incorporation of these territories in the Reich. German
sources report that it increased from 15·7 per cent. in
1938 to 22·0 per cent. in 1939 and 25·9 per cent. in 1940.
This is attributed partly to the introduction of the
German marriage-loan system, partly to the presence of
number of German troops. It dropped again to 20·8
per cent. in 1941.

As regards the death rate in the same area, information
is contradictory. According to some sources it has

remained practically the same : 14·2 in 1938, 13·9 in
1939, 14·3 in 1940, whilst according to other sources
there is an increase of 20 per cent. in the general death
rate and 50 per cent. in infant mortality.

In the Protectorate the birth rate has also increased,
from 14·3 per cent. in 1938 to 14·7 per cent. in 1939 and
16·8 per cent. in 1940. But the same source which
speaks of a steady death rate in the Sudeten territory
shows a definite worsening of the situation in the Protectorate, e.g., 12·5 per cent. in 1938, 13·0 per cent. in
1939 and 13·4 per cent. in 1940. The general death rate
remained on the same level in 1941 but infant mortality
rose from 9·4 per cent. in 1940 to 9·9 per cent. in 1941.

Education

In the Protectorate not only have the Czech universities and high schools been closed, but also many
secondary and even elementary schools. According to a
Decree of August 4, 1941, the elementary schools consist
now of two grades for children from 6 to 10 and from
11 to 14 years of age. The secondary schools were suppressed and replaced by Hauptschulen, to which only a
limited number of selected pupils is admitted at the
age of 10 plus.

German has been made compulsory from the third
school year and must be taught ' without giving the
pupils the impression that they are learning a foreign
language '. Furthermore, the Minister of Education
decided that as from the second term of the current
school year (1942) classes with more than 35 pupils
should be divided into two groups for learning German.
In the fourth and fifth forms German is to be taught
four hours a week, in the sixth, seventh and eighth forms
six hours a week ; in the Hauptschulen seven hours a
week. This has been made possible by curtailing the
time given to religious instruction, the Czech language,
History and Gymnastics. (*Venkov*, February 25, 1942.)

The Christmas holidays, which usually lasted 10 to
14 days, were extended in the winter of 1941–2 from
December 1 to March 30 in order to save fuel. Children
had to assemble at their schools once a week to be given

homework. The number of young people training for the teaching profession has been drastically curtailed.

In the Sudeten territory, all Czech schools have been closed. As in Germany, school children must help on the land, collect for the Winter Relief, etc. In Slovakia it is reported that the Slovakian Minister of Education finds the number of 50 grammar schools excessive for his small country and intends to reduce their number. Parents complain of their children being too much engaged outside the school and criticise the physical exercises, at which the children catch cold. (*Slovak*, March 3, 1941.)

Behaviour

As a result of unhappy incidents all school children are forbidden, by an order of the Minister of Education, to be in the streets after 8 p.m. unless accompanied by their parents. They may visit cafés only during the day-time and accompanied by parents or guardians. They may go to cinemas, concerts or theatres in the evening, but must go home immediately afterwards and be able to produce an identity card and the entertainment ticket. (*Der Neue Tag*, February 6, 1942.)

Youth Movements

The world-famous Sokols, the Scouts and all other Czech recreational and youth organisations have been dissolved. For German children, enrolment in the Hitler Youth is compulsory.

III. AMELIORATIVE MEASURES

There seems to have been little interference with most of the social services and institutions. Some will, however, require drastic reform and reorganisation after the war, others will not be difficult to restore once they are in proper hands.

As was seen in the previous section, schools of every type, elementary, secondary and vocational, have either been closed down or greatly reduced in their size and scope. All universities have been closed. It must therefore be assumed that after several years' interruption of all higher, academic and scientific education and skilled vocational training, there will be a serious shortage of young people in all professions and in all callings for which at least a secondary education is necessary. This will certainly be the case in the medical profession, and the suppression by one means or another of all Jewish doctors will further have a serious effect on medical services.

The lack of qualified young people will be felt also in the teaching profession. The first stage of reconstruction in this sphere will be, not only the utilisation of elderly teachers and masters and of those who have not been employed for many years past, but the provision of special courses to help those who have not been able, owing to the German occupation, to pass their final examination or to finish their studies. It will be necessary to help them to qualify within as short a time as possible.

Yet another urgent task will be the preparation of text-books for all types of schools to replace those that have been destroyed.

The supervision of health and the provision of holi-day-care and convalescent homes will need to be closely dovetailed with education, so that the generation weakened by the sufferings of war and the German occupation may have rapid and abundant help to restore its physical wellbeing.

DENMARK *

I. GENERAL CONDITIONS

In considering conditions here described account must be taken of the fact that there has been less interference in Danish Home Affairs by the occupying Power than in any other occupied country.

On December 31, 1939, the population of Denmark was estimated at 3,824,600, 922,000 or 24·1 per cent. being children under 14.

---

* Most of the information included in this chapter has been kindly furnished by the Information Office of the Danish Council in London.

General Economic Conditions

Nevertheless conomic life is being seriously affected by German occupation. Thus, the Danish Minister of Agriculture, K. Bording, in a speech to small landowners, said (April 21, 1942) :

> ' We sap our soil ; we sell our livestock and our stocks disappear. Our forests are over-drastically thinned and our bogs are plundered. We neglect normal building and repairs. In two years, prices of butter and eggs have risen by 90 per cent., pork by 40 per cent., cattle by 150 per cent. and barley by 70 per cent.'

Livestock has had to be reduced owing to the cessation of imports of fodder and fertilisers. The number of pigs has fallen from 3·2 million before the invasion to 1·1 on May 1, 1942 ; that of poultry from 32 million to 9 million in July 1941. Cattle were reduced by about 700,000 head to some 2,600,000, which is only a small decline and reflects the reluctance of farmers to spoil their excellent breeding stocks, which have been built up with such care over a long period. The milk yield during 1941 fell by 24 per cent. owing to scarcity of fodder.

Since the publication of the figures given above, the economic situation has worsened. The Danish Press now speaks openly about the serious effects of the economic situation on the country's standard of living. On April 1, 1942, a prominent provincial paper said that the lower standard of living imposed on the country, a fact hitherto unthinkable in agricultural Denmark, represented a threat to the health of the people. Food, clothing and fuel, it was said, were available only in insufficient quantities.

Danish exports to Germany are organised on the clearing system but the balance in favour of Denmark rose from 71 million kroner from May 1, 1940, to 988 million kroner on July 1, 1942. To this must be added the account of the Army of Occupation, *i.e.*, 1,036 million kroner on July 1, 1942, a grand total of 2,024 million kroner or £100 million.

On April 27, 1942, the Minister of Agriculture announced in the Danish Parliament that reports received

from experts showed that 76 per cent. of all wheat fields
would have to be completely ploughed up and resown
and that 12 per cent. needed to have additional grain
sown.   Only 12 per cent. of the whole area under wheat
promised a moderate yield.   Only 69 per cent. of the
acreage under rye was in good condition ; 15 per cent.
would have to be ploughed up and 16 per cent. to have
more grain sown.   An article in *Politiken* of May 1, 1942,
stated that the present ration of bread would be assured,
in spite of probably deficient crops of wheat and rye, by
the addition of barley to the flour.

Denmark's economic life is affected not only by the
imports of fooder and fertilisers for agriculture and by
the excessive sale of home-produced foodstuffs to
Germany, but also by the greatly reduced imports of
raw materials, particularly of coal, which touches both
home and industrial life, and by the decrease of rolling-
stock on the railways.   The Danish railways stated, for
instance, that as from April 21, 1942, they could no
longer accept ordinary freight goods.   Sea fishing is
handicapped by the shortage of fuel oil.

In January and February 1942, the unemployment
figures reached 197,000, in spite of a fairly extensive programme of public works, mainly roads, bridges, etc.
These public works have involved the movement of a
few thousand workers.   In September 1941, 28,895 Danes,
including 3,576 women, were reported by the *Reichsarbeitsblatt* to be working in Germany, and it is estimated
that their number reached between 35,000 and 40,000
in July 1942.

Food

Many fewer commodities are rationed in Denmark than
in most other European countries, but the consumption
of most goods, with the exception of potatoes, has been
much reduced as compared with pre-war standards.   In
April, according to the *Berlingske Tidende*, there was no
margarine and fats were in short supply.

The reduction in calories per person and per day is
shown in the following table.   This deficiency is, of course,
unequally distributed and the poorer families suffer more
severely.

Calories

Butter	250	(45 grammes available against 75 to 80 consumed before the war.)
Sugar	100	
Meat	100	(Supplies down by 20 per cent.; sometimes as much as 60 to 70 per cent. in towns.)
Milk	50	(In Copenhagen, in March, supplies came down to 10 per cent. of normal owing to transport difficulties.)
Cheese Eggs }	50	

Total loss 550

Increased consumption is registered in potatoes and certain other foods as follows :

Potatoes   100
Other foods 75

Total gain   175

leaving a daily average deficit of 375 calories or about 13·4 per cent.

For table of rationed foods see Appendix.

Clothing

According to the *Stockholm Tidningen* of March 26, 1942, the shortage was then becoming serious. Garments are rationed to some extent ; standard shoes and clothes have been introduced and the quality is said to be good. The prices are controlled (suits 100 kroner, socks 2·50 kroner, shoes 28 kroner).

Soap

One cake per month.

Fuel

Owing to reduced imports there is a serious shortage of fuel and the price is estimated at from 20 to 30 per cent. higher than in the winter of 1939–40. In towns, during the winter of 1941–42, each family received 55 bushels of solid imported fuel, while country people had to depend on home-produced fuel such as peat.

Medical Supplies

These are sufficient. The gathering of herbs has been organised.

II. EFFECTS OF WAR CONDITIONS ON CHILDREN

Health

On April 1, 1942, *Politiken* wrote : ' Rationing and the long, severe winter have caused hardship to children, who are suffering more than usual from colds and infectious diseases. Tuberculosis is undoubtedly on the increase; cases having been diagnosed in several schools, but official figures are not available. Teachers declare that undernourished children are often so devitalised that they have no appetite for the free meals provided in school.'

In February 1942, Dr. G. Jörgensen, Chief Medical Officer of Health, published in *National Tidende* the weight and height of all first-form pupils in his district for the following school years :

	Above average		Below average	
	Boys	*Girls*	*Boys*	*Girls*
1934–35 ..	12·9	12·1	20·4	9·4
1938–39 ..	12·5	9·8	19·8	10·4
1939–40 ..	11·4	10·3	23·0	10·9
1940–41 ..	11·5	9·5	24·0	10·9
1941–42 ..	10·7	7·2	25·8	12·5

It appears from these figures that the number of boys and girls above average weight and height is reported to be smaller in 1942 than in any previous year. Deterioration is also reflected in the average number of days' absence per scholar, which was 13·1 in 1934–35 and 14·2 in 1940–41. Dr. Jörgensen, commenting on these figures, says that they must be regarded as representing the starting point of a deterioration in the health of school children, the cause of which is to be seen in the lower standard of living and hygienic conditions.

Of the children medically examined in Odense in 1939, 12·29 per cent. were found to be under normal weight. In 1940 the percentage had risen to 14·03 and in 1941 to 16·36.

Dr. Aage Bojesen, in an interview published in the *Berlingske Tidende* of April 12, 1942, stated that the poorer families had suffered much from the cold. Children's wards in hospitals were crowded with children suffering from diseases caused by the cold, the unheated rooms and the lack of warm clothing. If warm clothing could have been provided many lives might have been saved.

Denmark, normally so clean, suffered during the winter from a plague of lice, which affected many schools, and provincial towns have had to establish public delousing centres. These vermin are said to have been brought back by German soldiers from the Eastern Front.

Vital Statistics

In 1940 the birth rate and the general death rate were still normal.

				Live Births	Deaths
1938	..	..	..	18·1	10·3
1939	..	..	..	17·8	10·1
1940	..	..	..	18·3	10·4

No figures are yet available for 1941, but the Danish wireless announced in July 1942, that infant mortality had increased from 5 per cent. to 5·5 per cent.

Education

There is not much to report under this heading as there has been little German interference. A number of new and modern schools, however, have been commandeered by the occupying army for military purposes. The severe winter, combined with the fuel shortage, compelled a number of schools to close for periods of varying length.

The National-Socialist *Faedrelandet* refers to a circular of the Minister of Education requiring teachers to use their authority over their pupils to prevent their molesting and sneering at their National-Socialist schoolmates.

Family Life

The fact that 30,000 to 40,000 Danish workers, many of whom are married, have been forced to seek employment in Germany or Norway has broken up a number of Danish families, but no details are available.

Juvenile Delinquency

It is reported that general criminality had increased by approximately 33 per cent. in 1941, but it is not said to what extent this increase affects juveniles.

On February 19, 1942, the *Aalborg Amts Tidende* reported that a growing number of quite young Copenhagen girls disappear from their homes and when found by the police are often full of vermin and infected with venereal diseases. Such cases of disappearance increased by 40 per cent. during 1941 as compared with 1940. Many other papers speak of the lowered morals of young people and the Danish women's associations have requested the Chief of the State Police to employ more policewomen for the control of young people, especially girls, in streets and restaurants.

Youth Organisations

Although a new National-Socialist youth organisation has been started on the model of the Hitler Youth, the old associations such as the Boy Scouts, the Girl Guides, the Boys' Brigade, the youth organisations of the Conservative, Social Democratic and Liberal Parties, as well as numerous sports associations for the young, are still very active and are now doing much to keep up the spirits of the young.

III. AMELIORATIVE MEASURES

So far as is known, pre-war welfare, health and educational services continue to function unchanged. There is no information about any new measures having been taken, although it must be assumed that adjustments have been made to meet war-time requirements.

FRANCE

NOTE.—This chapter was written before the occupation, by Germany, of " Unoccupied " France in November 1942.

I. GENERAL CONDITIONS

By the Armistice of June 1940, France was divided into two zones : the Occupied Zone and the Unoccupied Zone.

The Vichy Government nominally administers both zones, with the following exceptions :

(a) Alsace-Lorraine—incorporated in the Reich and administered like the rest of Germany.

(b) Flanders and Artois—linked to a ' Government of the Northern Provinces '. This Government has its seat at Brussels and includes the whole of Belgium, as well as French Flanders.

(c) The Prohibited Zone—consists of the whole coastal belt of the English Channel and Atlantic sea-board, to the frontier of Spain. Here, military authority is absolute, and the civil population which fled in May–June 1940 has not, as a rule, been allowed to return.

In the Unoccupied Zone, as in the Occupied, none of the decisions of the Vichy Government can be put into force until they have received the assent of the Occupying Authorities. These have their representatives in each Ministry and in each head office of Departmental and Local Government.*

Unless otherwise specified, the information recorded below applies to both Occupied and Unoccupied Zones.

Population

The total population of France, including Alsace-Lorraine, was estimated in 1936 at 41,300,000, of whom 10,400,000 were children under 15, and in 1941 at 41,270,000, of whom 9,540,000 were children under 15.

In April 1941 there were in 87 departments (Alsace-Lorraine excluded) 39,300,000 persons entitled to ration cards ; about 25 millions are assumed to be living in the Unoccupied Zone and 14 millions in the Occupied.

Present Economic Situation

I   *Agriculture*

Before the war France was nearly self-supporting as regards food, save for the produce of tropical and sub-tropical climates, such as coffee, etc.† The industrial and rural populations were fairly well balanced, but both

---

* See ' The Carving up of France', by René Cassin in *Entente*, London 1942.

† See Problems of Food Supply in France, *International Labour Review*, February 1942.

industry and agriculture were specialised regionally, so that when the two parts of the country were severed, the Unoccupied Zone was cut off from its main sources of supply for coal, textile goods, sugar-beet, wheat, potatoes, meat and dairy products.   The Unoccupied Zone consists for the most part either of mountainous districts, areas of rather poor soil which were used for cattle-breeding and for varied crops, or of extensive vineyards. There is also some fruit and vegetable growing in this Zone, but it did not produce in peace time more than one-third of the total of essential foodstuffs.   Since 1941 vine-growers have been obliged to grow other crops, mainly potatoes, on 10 per cent. of their land, but this does not seem yet to have improved the situation very greatly.   In many cases seed potatoes were either supplied too late or were eaten by the hungry peasants.   There seems also to be a certain amount of requisitioning, and there is probably some departmental selfishness, authorities trying to keep as much as they can in their own administrative area.   The 1940 crops suffered from war conditions, but those of 1941 were considerably better, amounting probably to 80 per cent. of the pre-war figure ; yet the food situation deteriorates steadily.   Black-marketing, hoarding and forging of coupons are frequently blamed.   There are no definite statistics of the amount of goods consumed by the army of occupation in France, nor of the amount sent to Germany.   It is believed to be high and a main cause of the present shortage, although the diminished trade with colonies and overseas countries and the lack of means of transport is a strongly contributing factor.   The absence of nearly two million young or fairly young men retained in captivity must also hamper production.

II   *Industry*

The equipment of many factories has been carried away to Germany, whilst most of the other factories can only work in so far as they are supplied with raw materials by Germany, which means that they work mainly on orders for Germany, and are able to produce very little for home consumption.

III *Unemployment*

In November 1941 the unemployed in both zones totalled 997,800. According to other information, however, the actual number of unemployed was much higher, as high indeed as one million, since many did not register, either because they belonged to trades and professions for which no relief is provided or because they did not want to attract attention. For instance, members of the professions, people dismissed for political or racial reasons, wives of men who had secretly left the Occupied for the Unoccupied Zone or to escape abroad, did not register.

IV *Cost of Living*

Prices have risen steeply, especially the prices of non-rationed goods. Dr. Bezançon, in a radio talk on October 15, 1941, declared that the cost of living had risen by from 60 per cent. to 150 per cent., without salaries being in proportion.

According to the *Bulletin de la Statistique générale* the increase on some retail prices in Paris from September raised 1939 to September 1941 was as follows :

Bread	—	Sugar	11 per cent.
Milk	60 per cent.	Meat (Beef)	33–44 per cent.
Cheese	20 per cent.	Coal	15 per cent.

Certain calculations show how disproportionate are salaries and the cost of living. In February 1941, for instance, in order to live fairly decently, if very modestly, a family of three required about 1,400 francs a month, but the official average salary for the department was 800 francs. One cause of low wages is the fact that some factories (mainly textile) work only 15 to 30 hours a week owing to lack of raw materials, so that workers paid by the hour bring home very small pay packets.

It has been calculated that the cost of rationed foods amounted in 1941 to about 5 francs per day, but that to have reasonably enough to eat it was necessary to spend in addition about 35 francs daily on unrationed or black-market foods. Few manual workers earn more than 1,200 francs a month and few clerks over 1,500 francs.

The mother of a family whose husband is a prisoner of war receives only 7 francs per day per child ; 8 to 10 francs if she is a refugee from the Occupied Zone ; clearly it is impossible to feed her family adequately. Nor can she buy clothing, since a pair of child's shoes costs at least 200 francs.

Movements of Population

The tragic flight across the country of millions of people from Belgium and Northern France is still in the minds of all. The total number has been estimated at from eight to ten millions, plus about 1,200,000 Belgians and some tens of thousands from Holland and Luxemburg. Many were caught by the advancing wave of the invading armies, some only at a few hours' distance from their homes. These were, of course, the first to go back to their homes, quite often on foot, as they had left them. Those who reached the Unoccupied Zone (about three and a half million French and 650,000 Belgians) arrived there in complete physical and mental exhaustion, having lost on the road most of the belongings they had tried to save. Their repatriation took about four months. Many could or would not be repatriated, some because their homes were in Alsace-Lorraine or in the ' forbidden zone ', some for political or racial reasons ; particularly in the case of people of Jewish origin. About 400,000 left their homes in Alsace-Lorraine after the armistice and arrived in the Unoccupied Zone just as the burden of the war refugees was beginning to ease. Some were expelled from Alsace-Lorraine at short notice and were only able to take with them a very limited amount of money and luggage.

Efforts are being made to provide homes and work for these refugees who cannot be repatriated, but it can well be understood that under present conditions it is far from easy. In the meantime they receive a daily relief allowance of :

10 to 15 francs per single person.
6 to 10   ,,   ,, married person.
7 to 12   ,,   ,, child.

A good many families, it seems, are still without permanent homes and the members are sometimes dispersed.

At the beginning of the war the whole population of the Eastern frontier region, including the 200,000 in-

habitants of Strasburg, had been compulsorily evacuated
to the centre of France, where they set up new com-
munities with administrative, social and medical services,
schools, etc., within the existing local community.

Food

Nominally, the rations are the same in the Occupied
and Unoccupied Zones, but the conditions vary very
greatly in different regions, in some one food stuff being
generally available and in others not. We have little
precise information on this but adult rations are estimated to be not more than 1,100 calories per diem.

It is valuable to compare the pre-war average consumption of standard foods with the present nominal
rations :

	Pre-War Average Grammes	Nominal Rations Grammes
Bread and flour ..	520 per day	275 per day
Sugar	2,000 per month	500 per month
Meat	3,600 ,, ,,	500 to 650 ,, ,,
Potatoes.. ..	10,000 ,, ,,	2,000 to 8,000 ,, ,,
Fats	1,000 ,, ,,	400 ,, ,,
Cheese	610 ,, ,,	200 ,, ,,
Coffee	390 ,, ,,	140 (substitute)

For table of rationed foods nominally available, see
Appendix.

Clothing

There has been some point-rationing since July 1941,
following a complete interruption of sales of clothing, but
it applies only to underwear and there is very little in the
shops to buy. Those who want an outer garment or a
pair of shoes must get a permit from the Town Hall
and prove that the goods are urgently needed. They
must also give up two old suits or other woollen articles
before they can obtain a new one. Repairing and
mending are made extremely difficult by the fact that
sewing-thread and mending-wool and cotton have been
very scarce ever since the summer of 1940. The repairing of worn-out shoes is a great problem.

It is almost impossible to get any new articles of
bedding.

Soap

Soap is very scarce and of poor quality.

Fuel

Very scarce, but locally rationed. At Lyons—to give one example—the following quantities were allowed for the period December 15, 1941, to January 15, 1942 :

Households of 1 to 3 persons ..   150 kilogrammes (3 cwt.)
  ,,   ,, 4 to 5   ,,   .. 225   ,,   (4½ cwt.)
  ,,   ,, 6 to 7   ,,   .. 300   ,,   (6 cwt.)
  ,,   ,, 12 persons or more 525 ,,   (10½ cwt.)

Additional allowances for families without gas and for families with young children :

Families with 1 child under 1 year   .. 50 kilogrammes (1 cwt.)
  ,,   ,, 1 child aged 1 to 5 years.. 25   ,,   (½ cwt.)
  ,,   ,, 2 children under 6 years.. 50   ,,   (2 cwt.)

The nominal rations were often not obtainable ; in Nice, for instance, and other southern districts which did not normally stock coal.

According to the *Petit Journal* of June 14, 1942, there is to be uniform rationing throughout the country, but the amount has not yet been fixed.

Medical Supplies

There are many drugs that cannot be obtained; others only in very limited quantities. There is also a lack of bottles and the complete disappearance of all rubber goods.

II.   EFFECTS OF WAR CONDITIONS ON CHILDREN

Nutrition, Health, and Growth

Complaint is general in every area that the population is underfed, that adults have lost 5 to 25 kilogrammes in weight, and that even if children have lost less the loss is even more serious in their case.

M. Caziot, the Vichy Minister for the Interior at that time, is reported to have declared on November 19, 1941, that all pupils in secondary schools had lost weight in 1940–41.

Conclusions to be drawn from a survey covering the year 1940 and the first eight months of 1941 were formulated in December 1941 by the National Children's Committee.*   At that time babies and young children had, on the whole, suffered less than school children and

------

* *Bulletin de l'Union in.ernationale de Secours aux Enfants,* Geneva.   Vol. VI.   No. 1–5.

young people. There were exceptions to this generalisation, for in the Lille area the young children seemed much more affected than in the rest of France. In that area, there was a good deal of under-nutrition, many premature births, numerous cases of broncho-pneumonia, furunculosis (boils), phthyriasis (an affection of the skin) and, in the poorer families, an uncommon amount of scabies. Infant mortality up to two years of age was double what it had been in preceding years. Even among families of skilled workers the growth and weight of babies remained well under the normal average, whether they were breast- or bottle-fed. It was mainly in cities that the growth and weight of young people was affected. Cases of tuberculosis had not increased in number but were of a more serious character.

Reporting on that survey at the Académie de Médécine (*Journal des Débats*, February 2, 1942) the well-known Doctors Huber, Colleson and Rouèche gave some further facts. There were few typical deficiency diseases but a great many troubles due to lack of organic balance. This was due not only to the general insufficiency of food but still more to the great deficiency of body-building foods. In Paris, in June 1941, medical examination of pupils from 14 to 16 years old showed only 20 per cent. as normally developed and gaining weight, 60 per cent. showing no change and 20 per cent. having lost weight.

According to *L'Effort* of December 20, 1941, the children of a large city of the Unoccupied Zone had lost weight in the following proportion :

90 per cent. in the elementary schools.
50 per cent. on the private schools.
5 per cent. in the lycées and secondary schools.

The difference between the groups is explained by the fact that the parents of the children of the third group are generally in a position to buy food in the black market and, therefore, to feed their children more generously.

Medical examination of children who were leaving for holiday camps showed an increase of 90 per cent. in tuberculosis or pre-tuberculosis cases.

An inquiry made in April and May 1941 at Marseilles among 84 families belonging to three income groups did not show marked differences between them. There was at the time: (a) a general deficiency in calories (1,800 per day instead of 2,500); (b) a deficiency in vitamin A, mainly in adults and young people ; in vitamin C, mainly in adults ; in vitamin D, very marked in younger children (54 per cent. among children under two years of age) and less in school children (10 per cent.). There was an iron deficiency of 10 per cent. in children under two, and X-ray examination showed some rickets in 40 per cent. of them. There was no hypo-albumen and no protein deficiency ; 10 per cent. of the children under two had lost weight, 22 per cent. of the children between two and twelve, 24 per cent. of the young people and 39 per cent. of the adults.

Another inquiry made at the same time among 144 school children divided into two income groups showed more caloric and vitamin deficiencies in the lower income-group ; 20 per cent. to 25 per cent. of the children showed decalcification of the bones. The vitamin deficiencies in the blood were revealed by laboratory tests, the health of the children not being apparently affected as yet.

Various reports speak of the lower weight of babies at birth. Discussing this point in March, the Académie de Médecine attributed it mainly to the fact that the addi-tional foodstuffs allocated to pregnant women are often eaten by other members of the family. (*Le Jour*, March 12, 1942.)

In March 1942, Carcopino, the State Secretary for National Education and Youth, sent to teachers a circular urging them to avoid all overwork for children. He said that, in view of the present conditions of heating and feeding and their effect upon intellectual and physical effort, the lives of children should be arranged with great care in order to avoid injuring their health and growth. The school time-table was to be reduced to an indis-pensable minimum. During open-air exercises, children were not to be made to strip from the waist up, or to do exercises that were too tiring or prolonged. Up to ten years, they were to have 11 hours' sleep. They should have a long rest on Thursdays and Sundays. (*Le Républicain du Gard*, March 14, 1942.)

As early as November 1941, school was to begin from half to one hour later in the morning, physical training and sports were reduced from five to three hours per week for boys and from four to two hours for girls. (*Havas News Agency*, November 26, 1941.)

The previous data refer to conditions about a year ago, and they are said to be worse since the winter of 1941–42, when rations were much lower than the preceding winter and when possible reserves in the family had been exhausted. People travelling in France during the spring of 1942 speak with deep concern of the obviously debilitated health of children and adults, while Swiss people are very much impressed by the poor appearance of children invited to their country to recuperate. We have not been able to get any statistical evidence in support of these reports.

On March 12, 1942, the Académie de Médecine expressed the hope that if possible all pupils should have distributed to them an additional daily ration of 300 to 400 calories. (*Le Jour*, March 12, 1942.)

Diseases

The French and the Occupying Authorities alike keep close watch over epidemic diseases and, so far, there has been no increase. On February 11, 1942, Radio-Lyons urged people to get re-vaccinated as a few cases of smallpox had been reported in the Paris area. Rumours of an epidemic of typhus in the same region were denied, and the number of typhoid fever cases was stated to be within the average.

Concern is felt about an increase of pulmonary tuberculosis among young people and also about an increase of venereal diseases (the latter due to an increase in juvenile prostitution and to lack of specific drugs). No precise figures are given.

Vital Statistics

The influence of the war on vital statistics is already very marked. The *Bulletin de la Statistique générale* records that from 1939 to 1940 :

    (a) The marriage rate had decreased by 32 per cent. (77,000 less in 1940 than in 1939).

    (b) The birth rate had decreased by 9 per cent.

(c) The general death rate had increased by 18 per cent.

(d) The infant mortality rate had increased by 48 per cent. (from 6·3 per cent. in 1939 to 9·1 per cent. in 1940).

(e) The excess number of deaths over births had increased by 47·6 per cent.

The decrease in the marriage rate and birth rate can be easily explained when it is remembered that about 140,000 men (including civilians) have been killed, and that about three million others are prevented from marrying and procreating by being retained in captivity (two millions), by enrolment in labour or youth camps (200,000), or in the army (200,000), by having gone abroad (300,000) or by separation from their families for other causes. Further, many married people voluntarily refrain from bringing children into the world because of their precarious position and economic difficulties.

In 1940 there was a total of 735,000 deaths, including 17,000 civilian war casualties—an increase of 18 per cent. over 1939 (642,000 in 1936). Deaths among children and old people were 48,760 as compared with 36,742 of the same age group in 1939.

During the first five months of 1941, the death rate was increased by :

(a) 10 per cent. among children under 14.

(b) 22 per cent. among persons between 14 and 60 years of age.

(c) 43 per cent. among persons over 60.

Medical reports from Paris published in *The Times* of November 10, 1941, show the death rate of the new-born to have been 17 per cent. higher in the first half of 1941 than in the corresponding period of 1938. This increase was due more to exposure to cold, since houses were practically unheated, than to insufficient or inadequate food.

In February 1942, mortality in the Paris region was 37·9 per cent. higher than in February 1941, and 53 per cent. higher than before the war (*Svenska Dagbladet*, May 29, 1942).

Education

With the exception of Alsace-Lorraine, where the Germans have taken over the schools, education is more or less continued on the same basis, especially in the elementary schools. The Vichy Government professes to lay more stress on religion than formerly, and to prepare the young more deliberately for family life. As a matter of fact, only a limited number of teachers has been dismissed, while lack of paper prevents the printing of new text-books to accord with the views of the Vichy Government.

It was intended to lay more stress on physical training, but the poor stamina of the children makes this hardly possible.

Free secondary education is abolished but scholarships are to be given to talented children. The ' écoles primaires supérieures ' are abolished and children are to attend either a ' lycée ', where education is mainly based on the classics, or a ' collège ' where instruction will be based on science and modern languages and include technical subjects and agriculture ; this after an examination at 11 years of age. The children remaining in the primary schools will not be able to take their final examination before 14 years of age, a measure aimed at preventing the cleverer children from leaving school before that age, sometimes before 13 years of age.

Changes have been introduced in the recruitment and training of elementary school teachers. The ' écoles normales ' are abolished and prospective teachers will have to go through the ' lycées ' and from there to ' instituts de formation professionelle '.

Family Life

There is inevitably disintegration of family life when so many families are without the father, or are separated, some members living in the Occupied and others in the Unoccupied Zone, but it has not been possible to obtain any precise information.

Behaviour and Social Adjustment

In a speech at a meeting of the ' Conseil supérieur de l'Administration pénitentiaire et des Services de l'Education surveillée ', M. Joseph Barthélemy (' Garde des

Sceaux '), stated that juvenile delinquency was increasing
markedly. He did not, however, give any figures and
said he was not in a position to define the real causes of
this deterioration. (*Le Temps*, September 30, 1941.)

This increase is particularly noticeable in the larger
cities of the Unoccupied Zone, but the large influx of
refugees has so swelled the former population that no
comparison with pre-war conditions can reasonably be
made. Even in relatively small towns, however, the
number of cases brought before the Juvenile Courts has
increased considerably ; *e.g.*, Macon (19,000 inhabitants) :
27 cases in 1938, 38 in 1939, 62 in 1940 and 32 in the first
three months of 1941 ; Châteauroux (26,000 inhabitants):
37 cases in 1938, 137 in 1940.

Among the many causes are certainly the prolonged
absence of many fathers as prisoners of war, the consequent anxiety, depression and sometimes demoralisation
of the mother, and the amount of time she must spend
queueing for food and other necessities. For many children
the adventurous life they had as refugees, sleeping anywhere and eating whatever they could lay their hands on,
has had an anti-social effect.

There are complaints also of the increasing number of
quite young girls (15 to 16) giving birth to illegitimate
children or becoming prostitutes.

Juvenile Employment

We have no information about the employment of
children and young people.

In both zones are to be found ' youth centres ' which
cater for the needs of the young unemployed (14 to 20
years old). The Swedish *Dagens Nyheter*, of December
19, 1941, mentions 250 such centres catering for 15,000
young people in the Unoccupied Zone and 25,000 in the
Occupied Zone.

Recreation and Youth Organisations

All youth organisations are forbidden in the Occupied
Zone at present. In the Unoccupied Zone, however,
great importance is attached to them.

---

* ' Abandon moral et délinquance,' by Abbé Jean Plaquevent in
Bulletin de l'Union internationale de Secours aux Enfants, 1942,
Vol. VI, No. 1–5.

Pre-war organisations like the Scouts, the J O C
(Christian Young Organisation) and others have greatly
increased their numbers. Early in 1942, these totalled
about 500,000 members. The Scouts alone have increased
in the past two years from 42,000 to 120,000. Only one
important new organisation has been created since the
armistice, the ' Compagnons de France ', for young
people from 15 to 25. In 1941 it had a membership of
about 30,000.

No attempt has been made to bring all young people
under one flag, a variety of organisations being considered
more likely to suit the needs of individual young people.
Camp schools to train leaders have been opened.

(Over and above the voluntary organisations and the
youth centres for unemployed mentioned above, a third
form of youth organisation, the youth-camps, ' Chantiers
de la Jeunesse ', takes young men of 20 years old for a
period of eight months and gives them some form of
physical and moral training instead of military con-
scription. For the most part they are employed on work
of public importance : canalisation of rivers, drainage
of swamps, forestry, making roads and mountain paths,
etc.)

III. AMELIORATIVE MEASURES

Welfare, Health and Education Services

Welfare, health, and education services do not seem
to have been much affected; but pensions paid, for
instance, to war widows and to dependants of prisoners
of war, seem quite inadequate in view of the present
cost of living.

The avowed policy of the Vichy Government is to lay
emphasis on family life and to try to increase the birth
rate. The ' Conseil supérieur de la Natalité ' and the
' Haut Comité de la Population ' were replaced on June
7, 1941, by a ' Comité consultatif de la Famille française '.
Family allowances were increased by a decree of November
18, 1940, and by a law of February 15, 1941. They
amount now to :

(a) 10 per cent. of the average departmental salary
for the second child.

(b) 20 per cent. of the average departmental salary for the third child.

(c) 30 per cent. of the average departmental salary for each successive child.

To these allowances may be added the ' one-salary allowance '—for families where only one of the parents is gainfully employed outside the home—viz. :

(a) 20 per cent. for an only child under 5.

(b) 10 per cent. for an only child over 5.

(c) 25 per cent. for two children.

(d) 30 per cent. for three or more children.

This latter allowance is only given to French children, whereas the family allowance is given to all families qualifying for it, without regard to nationality.

The first child entitles the mother to a grant, which is now double the amount of the average salary in the department. Half is paid at birth and half six months later. The child must be of French nationality, legitimate, and born within two years of the parents' marriage.

According to a law of August 14, 1942, a ' priority card ' is given to pregnant mothers and mothers of large families (four children under 16, or three under 14, or two under four) entitling them to priority in public offices, public conveyances, and shops.

A reduction of secondary school fees for children belonging to large families has now been extended to vocational and trade schools. The reduction amounts to 20 per cent. in the case of two children ; 30 per cent. in the case of four children ; 40 per cent. in the case of five children. The fee is entirely remitted for families of six or more. (*Havas News Agency*, March 24, 1942.)

The Ministry of Education comprises now three Secretaries. Those for (1) Public Instruction, (2) Fine Arts, (3) Youth ; as well as two General Commissioners dealing with (1) Youth Camps and (2) General Education and Sports.

Great emphasis is being laid on physical training and many new sports grounds have been or are being created —often connected with schools.

To make adoption easier the minimum age limit for adoptive parents has been lowered from 40 to 35 years

old, provided they have been married for at least ten
years and have remained childless.

Relief Measures

Some 500 decrees and orders have been passed relating
to the food supply. The entire organisation is assumed
by a State Secretary for Food Supply, working through
central offices, regional, departmental and local services,
and Buying Commissions. The work is mostly carried
out through the already existing services and staffs.

War relief is centralised by the ' Secours national ', a
semi-official organisation which draws its funds from
private gifts and collections, as well as from certain
luxury taxes. Early in 1942, the ' Secours national ' was
feeding about one million persons in its communal feeding
centres, as well as 800,000 children in school canteens.

Up to December 31, 1941, there were 4,600 kitchens and
school canteens, which had distributed 135 million meals,
at a cost of 290 million francs. There were in addition
3,637 canteens not at that time under the direction of
the ' Secours national ' which received subsidies for
22,610,000 francs.

Beyond the food provided in canteens, 8,000 tons of
casein-biscuits were distributed to 4,200,000 children and
86 millions of sweets containing vitamins were given to
2,845,000 children.

According to Radio Paris on March 4, 1942, out of
400,000 school children of the Seine, 150,000 had their
mid-day meal at school. The Préfecture was arranging
for more premises so as to increase the number.

As from February 8, 1942, the ' Secours national ' has
been supplying free of charge to pregnant and nursing
mothers vitamin B and C tablets (eight a week to each
mother) and to bottle-fed babies (four a week).

Foreign and international organisations are also trying
to alleviate distress.

For some time during the summer of 1941, gifts of the
American Red Cross made possible a daily distribution of
50 grammes of bread to children in the schools and also,
in some cities, a glass of milk (made with powdered milk).

Vitamins in the form of sweets have been distributed on several occasions in schools in urban centres.

The International Commission for the Relief of War Refugees, which had started its work in France early in 1939 on behalf of the Spanish War refugees, has extended it to all groups of war victims. Its work is now merged with that of the American Quakers. In April 1942, it was feeding 84,500 children ; it distributed vitamins to 100,000 children and had organised 16 colonies (camps) for 650 children. It sponsored many other activities from which adults, as well as children, benefited, especially in the internment camps for foreign refugees.

The Swiss Committee for the Relief of Child War Victims is providing additional food for children and running children's homes in France itself. It has also organised the reception of debilitated children in Switzerland for a few months' recuperation. Over 13,000 children from both zones had gone to Switzerland up to June 1942. Most of them have been received in families free of charge ; those with incipient tuberculosis or needing special attention for any other reason are cared for in convalescent homes.

The Save the Children International Union (Geneva) has on many occasions sent consignments of tinned milk, babies' foods, clothing, cheese and so on. It also helps individual children through its ' photocard ' scheme, supported by friends in Sweden and Switzerland.

The Joint Relief Commission of the International Red Cross (International Committee and League of Red Cross Societies) has, with funds supplied by the French Red Cross, bought and sent for distribution 500 tons of tinned milk, babies' foods, Ovaltine, pulses and dried vegetables, mainly to the Occupied Zone. Gifts from other organisations, chiefly from the Americas, have enabled the Commission to dispatch to both zones several consignments of milk foods for babies and children. Medical supplies have been sent to internment camps in the south of the country, but for lack of funds some of the food that was most needed could not be sent.

GREECE

I. GENERAL CONDITIONS

Greece is occupied by three different Powers :

i.   Western Thrace and Eastern Macedonia, occupied by Bulgaria ;

ii.   Some parts of Northern Greece, including Salonika, occupied by the Germans ;

iii.   The remainder of the mainland and the islands are nominally occupied by the Italians, but are, in fact, under the dual control of Italy and Germany.

According to the 1928 census the population of Greece numbered 6,204,700, of which 1,989,700 or 32·1 per cent. were under 15.

Present Economic Conditions

Normally two-thirds of all Greeks are employed in agriculture, but mainly in the cultivation of a few specialised crops, such as tobacco, grapes and olives. These were exported in large quantities, but in exchange Greece had always to import about 40 per cent. of its normal foodstuffs. Since part of the most productive agricultural land has been ravaged by the war or is being occupied by Bulgaria, home production is more than ever below the country's needs, and the situation is made more serious by the requisitioning for Germany of part of the wheat set aside for seed. Moreover, the peasants naturally try to deliver as little as possible of their produce to the Occupying Authorities and barter it privately against things they need. Since a large proportion of the olive oil was produced in Crete and many of the vineyards are in the islands, the mainland is suffering from a shortage even of its standard produce. Furthermore, coastal shipping has practically ceased and inland transportation (always of secondary importance in Greece) is hindered by the war-time destruction of communications and by the absence of fuel.

All stocks were, of course, requisitioned immediately after the occupation, while the German soldiers, every one of whom had received 50,000 drachmas' worth of paper money, bought all they could to send home to Germany, so that shops were soon empty of goods. The army of

D

occupation, too, has to be fed from the country, and it is reported that many German civilians also are coming to Greece. The almost total lack of raw material handicaps industry, as does also the absence of coal and electric power. Shipping, which was the chief source of the national revenue, has almost entirely ceased to provide work or revenue for Greece, since those ships which have not managed to escape and join the Allied fleets, are immobilised in harbours. As a consequence, unemployment in sea-coast and industrial towns is rife. It is reported that last summer at the harbour of Volo, for instance, out of a working population of 18,000, there were 12,000 unemployed. (*Bukarester Tageblatt*, July 7, 1942.)

The incidence of unemployment is also heavy in many other trades and professions as most industrial concerns, banks, etc., have been taken over by the Germans and many Greeks refuse to work for or under them. This is true also of those formerly employed on public works, such as road and bridge building.

The cost of living has increased so greatly that wages had to be raised by 110 per cent. to 140 per cent. between July and November 1941.

Movements of Population

The greatest movement of population is from the Bulgarian occupied territories into the rest of Greece. About 100,000 persons have been forced to leave Eastern Macedonia and Western Thrace : teachers, members of the liberal professions, traders and peasants whose holdings have been taken by Bulgarian settlers. In addition, many people who fled before the invasion have sought a refuge at Athens and a thousand families are said to have been expelled from Salonika alone by the Germans.

There is, naturally, a great effort made by the Occupying Authorities to recruit workers for Germany. *Transocean News Agency* reported on May 11, 1942, that 26,000 workers had already left Macedonia for Germany ; on June 2, it announced the departure of the 11th transport of such workers which, for the first time, included a number of men from Athens and Southern Greece.

Food

Of the 1,200,000 tons of wheat a year normally consumed (or nearly 3,300 tons a day), at least a third had
to be imported.

Already on October 14/15, 1941, the *Stockholms
Tidningen* published the following information :

For months the bread ration was under 200 grammes
(7 oz.) per person daily and was recently reduced to 100
grammes. One could obtain only the bread ration and
grapes. Now you cannot even get grapes and the last few
days I was in Athens there was hardly anything but
apples, even tomatoes being a great rarity and oil obtainable only on the black market. . . . In certain areas
such as Corinth, Patras, and various Ægean islands,
neither bread nor flour had been distributed for months.
Under normal conditions most of the people live on bread,
oil, onions, olives and goats' milk cheese, and an adult
will eat about 800 grammes of bread a day. Since
April 27 meat has been distributed about three or four
times—not per month, but over the whole period—and
even so only 100 to 150 grammes per person. During the
same period macaroni and rice were sold twice and sugar
only once. Coffee was sold in minute quantities, and
cheese, olives, raisins and potatoes have been issued two
or three times. That is all. One no longer sees queues
in the streets as the shops are empty and there is nothing
to queue for. On the official market there is nothing
available but a little fruit and sometimes, but nowadays
seldom, a few tomatoes and egg-plants. Famished people
rove around in the richer quarters and investigate the
garbage bins. One sees them stuff their mouths or
pockets with filth which even a stray dog would refuse.

Nothing definite is known about rationing. In March
and April 1942, the bread ration was said to be as low as
5 oz. four times a week and 2 oz. every second day, but
according to the *Donauzeitung* of May 5, it had been
raised to 80 drams (250 grammes or 9 oz.) four days a
week and left at 50 drams (150 grammes or 5 oz.) every
other day. Small quantities of other foodstuffs are
distributed very irregularly. There is a good deal of
activity on the black market but only a very small pro-

portion of the population can afford the extravagant prices. Conditions are assumed to be slightly better in the country but very little is known for certain. In March, in Salonika, the bread ration was stated by the *Transocean News Agency* to be 125 grammes (4 oz.) five times a week.

In a first-hand report, dated March 1942, and received by the Save the Children International Union, the situation is described as ' tolerable ' in nursery schools, but here is the daily fare of the children : ' In the morning a warm drink with sugar or with syrup of grapes, at midday a soup, or a " bouillon " (clear soup) with a little oil. They have meat only when the Police or the Ministry can get some, and that is very rarely '.

In this same report we read further : ' For 11 months no condensed or powdered milk has been imported. (These formed the main food for non-breast-fed babies, since fresh milk was never good or plentiful in towns.) Such milk-yielding animals as there are, being badly fed, no longer give as much milk as before and are mostly taken for butcher's meat. It is expected that there will soon be no milk at all.'

The worst period seems to have been during the intense cold of February ; since the arrival of foodships in the spring the situation is slightly better, as is proved by the increased bread ration and an increase in the supply of fresh vegetables and olive oil reported by *Transocean* on May 6. The ration of oil has been fixed at 75 drams (235 grammes or 8½ oz.) per month. (*Proimos Typos*, Athens, May 20, 1942.) *Athinaikanea* announced, on May 16, that fish would soon be distributed against ration cards and that the following week everybody would be entitled to one egg, costing 55 drachmas. There is also a small decrease in prices.

Clothing

Owing to the shortage of textiles, the manufacture of a standard cloth was announced by *Transocean* on August 24, 1942, with the statement that the manufacture of other cloth would not be allowed.

Soap

One small cake has been distributed once or twice during the whole period of the occupation. On May 5,

1942, *Kathimerini* announced that 75 grammes (2½ oz.) of soap per person would soon be distributed, for the first time in many months.

Fuel

Acute shortage. The supply of gas and electricity has been limited. It was even reported from Athens (*Donau-zeitung*, September 7, 1941) that, except for hospitals, gas was completely cut off at Athens.

Medical Supplies

Drugs are almost completely lacking. The shortage of quinine is especially serious in view of the prevalence of malaria, which affects 40 per cent. of the population. It used to be freely sold and in malaria-ridden districts the State distributed free of charge a specially strong preparation to all people who had had attacks of the disease, even months or years earlier. Quinine was distributed gratuitously in schools and training colleges, to recipients of State welfare subsidies, to members of peasant co-operatives, prisoners and many other groups of the community. Now it is supplied only on a doctor's prescription.

II. EFFECTS OF WAR CONDITIONS ON CHILDREN

Health

That the starvation suffered by the Greek population has tragically affected the lives and health of children is proved by the much-increased death-rate.

The following is an except from the report to the Save the Children International Union (March 1942):

' The records of the child welfare centres (Athens) show that children are losing weight badly—up to an average of 1 kilogramme (2¼ lb.) a month—through the almost total lack of milk. . . . Infant mortality has almost doubled and there is a painful apprehension that the moment when babies, now losing weight, will reach the stage of athrepsia (extreme emaciation) is approaching. When the heat of the summer comes the death-rate will be terrible.

Even greater dangers threaten the babies who are not brought to the centres, and it is now only too common to see in the streets of Athens mothers carrying babies in a condition of athrepsia ; sometimes already dead.

School children were so weak during the winter that the Government had to limit the number of lessons to three per day.

Diseases

The most prevalent diseases are stomach ulcers and other affections of the digestive organs, and tuberculosis and malaria. (*The Times,* April 15, 1942.) As far back as October 1941, *i.e.,* after only a few months of occupation and before the effects of famine were felt, a leading specialist on tuberculosis stated that the number of persons suffering from consumption had trebled.

During the winter of 1941–42, there was an epidemic of diphtheria at Athens.

In May 1942, the police ordered the closing of all theatres, cinemas, concert halls, cafés and schools, to protect the public against the spread of epidemics, especially of typhus, of which several cases had been reported. (*Transocean News Agency,* May 19, 1942.)

Vital Statistics

According to the official records in the municipal registers of Athens and the Piræus, the number of deaths for the four months October 1, 1941, to January 26, 1942, reached 30,000. But according to the Greek Red Cross this figure is inaccurate, since many families do not disclose the deaths in their homes in order that they may not be deprived of the ration cards of the dead. On the basis of special investigations, deaths during the above period should be reckoned to have reached, if not to have exceeded, the figure of 40,000, a great many of them among children. This is an average of 330 daily or eight times the normal pre-war figure. The peak seems to have been reached in February 1942 when foreign journalists reported that lorries collected dead bodies every morning from the streets, and that the Church had had to suspend its ban on cremation.

For the quarter August to October 1941, that is to say before the situation had become so severe, there were in six districts of the Athens-Piræus area 473 births, against

610 in the corresponding period of 1939, and 1,080 deaths against 392 in 1939.

The situation is reported to be as bad, if not worse, in other towns such as Salonika, Patras, Volo, etc., and in the islands, particularly Chios and Syra. The inhabitants of Syra are said to have wired to Athens : ' Send wheat or coffins '.

From August 1941 to March 1942, 320,000 deaths were registered in Greece, that is to say more than five times the normal death-rate. Live births are much reduced in number and very few newborn children survive. (Report from Istanbul to *The Times*, April 15, 1942.)

Education

Owing to the weak physical condition of the children and to the shortage of fuel, which made it necessary to close during the winter the few schools that were not requisitioned for other purposes, no regular education can be given to most children.

Moreover, very large numbers of teachers have been driven to manual work or transported to the war factories in Germany and Italy. An American newspaper even reported that educated persons who offered to teach elementary subjects on a voluntary basis were fined or imprisoned.

In such secondary schools as remained open there are attempts to inoculate the young with National-Socialist theories. Nevertheless, Poland and Greece were the only occupied countries which did not send representatives to the Weimar Youth Conference which met sometime ago.

In the area occupied by Bulgaria, all Greek schools have been closed. A Bulgarian school is reported to have been opened in Salonika.

Family Life and Dependency

The present circumstances have either knit the family closer, or else the family has been totally disintegrated by the death of one or both parents, by their imprisonment or by deportation.

It has been estimated that about 150,000 to 200,000 Greeks have died from execution, massacre or starvation. (*The Times*, March 17, 1942.) Villages have been burned down and many of the inhabitants massacred. For instance, the whole male population over the age of 16 of the village of Mesovotini were put to death in October 1941, comprising about 200 men and youths.

Further, in the report sent to the Save the Children International Union, it is stated :

' Many orphans or abandoned children of all ages are found wandering the streets (of Athens) near canteens or restaurants, dirty, starving, pale and thin, a sight recalling Dante. They stop at nothing to get a bit to eat ; searching among the refuse or fighting the dogs for something edible. The Patriotic Institute for Social Welfare and Relief tries to meet the situation. After a short period of medico-social supervision, the children are placed in families for a sum of 2,500 drachmas (approximately £4 4s.) per annum, plus the use of canteens, or in an establishment which was formerly a lunatic asylum but is now empty because all its inmates are dead.

' Adolescents are placed provisionally.

' The Institute has also been able to place about 1,000 children in the country and hopes that the number may soon be increased.

' A great many children of all ages have arrived from occupied Eastern Macedonia and Western Thrace. The refugees from these areas have been provisionally housed at Salonika, Volo, Chalkis and Athens. A great many orphaned or lost children have found shelter in the orphanages or have been placed in families. '

It is reported that very young girls have taken to prostitution in order to obtain food.

III. AMELIORATIVE MEASURES
Welfare, Health and Educational Services

These have not been interfered with by the Occupying Authorities, but activities have necessarily been curtailed owing to the general depression, the lack of money, and of transport. This is exemplified in the following extracts (March 1942) :

' During the past twelve months the number of pregnant women receiving advice through our Maternity Section has been less than in previous years—a decrease particularly noticeable since October 1941. This is shown

In the figures for five pre-natal centres in Athens for the second half of 1940 and of 1941 respectively :

July to December	Registered Cases	New Cases	Midwives' Domiciliary Visits
1940	898	541	1,358
1941	532	202	971

' In January and February 1942, the work seems to have slowed down even more. The causes are many : the absence of fathers, the almost total lack of foodstuffs, the entire lack of transport and the general distress.

' The Child Welfare Centres also have much less to do, there being fewer consultations for the same reasons.

' Through the medium of the Greek Red Cross, the International Red Cross has sent supplies of powdered milk,* the Patriotic Institute organised the distribution and 25,000 babies have already benefited. In March 1942, about 6,000 were still receiving milk, but the needs are far greater, especially since, because of under-nourishment, the mothers have not enough milk for adequate breast-feeding.

' The Institute distributes rice to babies in the Welfare Centres and to certain other cases medically certified (500 grammes, i.e., 18 oz. per baby per month) ; but the stock of rice in our dépôt is rapidly diminishing and will soon be exhausted.

' Clients have also become less numerous in the dispensaries. The mothers who formerly brought their children to the dispensary for the slightest reasons will come now only if absolutely forced by circumstances. Not only is the morale of the women very low, but the severe winter and the complete lack of all means of transport have added to the difficulties. Fortunately, apart from a small epidemic of diphtheria, the incidence of disease during the past half-year has been slight. The specialised dispensaries (anti-venereal, anti-trachoma) continue working almost normally.

' Holiday colonies and convalescent homes have not worked this past year, and as the buildings have been

---

* The Save the Children International Union contributed to one such contingent.

requisitioned it is improbable that they will be able to open within the near future.

' A children's hospital has been opened at Penteli, since the Army of Occupation requisitioned the Athens hospital.

' The provincial centres of the Patriotic Institute at Serres, Drama, Kavalia, Komotini, Alexandropolis, Kato-Neurokopi, have had to suspend work.'

The Ministry of Economics has authorised the opening of 50 nurseries for the children of land workers in Macedonia and Thrace, 15 in the Epirus and 25 in other parts of the country (*Eleftheron*, Vima, May 17, 1942.)

Relief

Families which are still better-off than their neighbours have adopted for the duration of the war one or two abandoned children, and either given them a home or taken them as guests for the two main meals of the day.

Apart from the milk and rice distributed to babies in its child welfare centres, the Patriotic Institute is occasionally able to organise soup kitchens with provisions sent by the International Red Cross. These, when open, are used by 2,000 children, three to six years old.

The International Red Cross, during the winter of 1941–42, sent also a certain amount of condensed milk, Ovaltine, ' Larosan' (a dietetic food that makes up in a certain measure for the lack of milk) and vitamin C. A train of truck-loads of tinned milk left Switzerland in April 1942.

The Occupying Authorities have had to take steps to ameliorate the situation. *Stefani News Agency* announced on April 23, that 6,000 tons of foodstuffs and 1,700,000 eggs had recently arrived in Greece from Serbia and Bulgaria and were to be used in the communal kitchens and for the children. The *Donauzeitung* reported on May 21, that the German authorities had supplied the Macedonian soup kitchens with 50 tons of beans and 50 tons of rice. Nevertheless, the main relief still comes from Allied sources.

From October 1941 to January 1942, a Turkish steamer, the Kurtulush, brought consignments of 1,500 tons of food and medicines from a reserve of 50,000 tons stored in Turkey by the Greek War Relief Association of

America. This reserve does not include any wheat. The
Kurtulush struck a reef and foundered on its sixth
voyage, and was replaced later by the Dulumpinar,
which carries 1,900 tons each time. These cargoes were
used to feed 500,000 people daily in the Athens-Piræus
area ; in May their number was increased to 600,000.
But the quality of food is low through lack of fats, each
portion containing less than 500 calories against the 2,500
of the rations distributed by the feeding centres in the
winter of 1940–41. (In the winter of 1939–40, the food
distributed in the same area did not exceed 135,000
meals daily.)

In addition to the Turkish steamers, two Swedish ships
chartered by the Red Cross brought cargoes of wheat,
flour, and medical supplies in March and April and one
cargo of 7,000 tons of wheat was sent from Syria in
March. In April 1942 an agreement was reached—but
not put into operation until August—concerning a monthly
shipment of 15,000 tons of Canadian wheat to the mainland, and early in May another agreement for the distribution of 500 tons of foodstuffs in the islands.

These cargoes are paid for by the Greek Government
and their distribution is supervised by delegates of the
International Red Cross.

LUXEMBURG*
I. GENERAL CONDITIONS

Luxemburg, invaded on May 10, 1940, was formally
incorporated into Germany on June 28 in the Province
(or ' Gau ') of Koblenz-Trier, which was renamed ' Gau
Moselland ' in February 1941.

Incorporation in the Reich meant, of course, that the
whole governmental administration of Luxemburg, as
of well as all public and private institutions, had to be
adapted to or absorbed in the corresponding German
services and institutions. Every effort is made to persuade
the population of its German character and of the
advantages that it will enjoy as part of the Reich.

---

* The information on Luxemburg is due almost entirely to the
kindness of Mr. Victor Bodson, Minister of Justice.

In spite of this, however, 98 to 99 per cent. of the inhabitants, at a census taken in October 1941, declared themselves to be of Luxemburg language and nationality. Investigations are now being made—with success, according to a report of Radio-Oslo on April 1, 1942—in order to establish the existence of ' Pure Germans ', and to register them under this heading.

The language commonly spoken is a German dialect, but French and German were equally recognised as official languages before the war. Since August 8, 1940, however, German is the only official language.

Luxemburg has a total population of about 300,000 of whom 63,113 or 21·37 per cent. are children under 15.

Present Economic Conditions

It appears that the economic situation in the Grand Duchy has deteriorated considerably since the invasion, although there is no unemployment because, according to the German economic laws introduced on February 27, 1942, workers are compelled to take up any kind of work at any place.

The Luxemburg iron and steel industry which, with a productive capacity of about three million tons, made Luxemburg the seventh largest steel-producing country in the world, has been entirely taken over by the Germans. Production is only about 25 per cent. of pre-war output owing to lack of coke, lime and manganese. There is also a great deal of passive resistance on the part of the workers, which contributes to the decreased output.

The transport situation is extremely grave. Many of the train services have been suspended, and the small amount of rolling stock still available is in a bad condition. Horses have also been widely requisitioned ; in some villages only two have been left for all services ; 30 per cent. of all cattle has been confiscated for slaughter. Forests have been cut down, and the wood transported to Germany.

Movements of Population

As in Belgium and France, many Luxemburgers fled before the invasion in May 1940, but later returned home. Now there are many men who try to escape in order to join the British and Allied Forces. No voluntary emigration of whole families can be reported, but the number of families compelled to leave their homes and their country is considerable.

In the industrial town of Rumelange (4,000 inhabitants) out of 800 miners, 700 have been deported to Germany and replaced by Spanish labour. Altogether 4,000 out of the 21,000 industrial workers of the Grand Duchy have been forced to take up work in Germany and it appears that at least 1,500 have left the country with their families, thus making room for German families to settle in their towns or villages. A great many members of the professional classes have lost their work because they refused to sign a declaration of adherence to the German Reich. Being unemployed, they have often been forced to take up manual labour, even of the heaviest kind, in Germany.

As in other occupied countries, mass deportations of Jews have taken place in Luxemburg. Some were taken as far as the Portuguese frontier, but a larger number were deported to Poland.

Food

Prior to the German invasion large stocks of foodstuffs, accumulated from the rich harvests of the years preceding the outbreak of war, were available in the Grand Duchy. These were requisitioned by the Germans in the first days after the invasion, as were most of the available cattle. Prices have risen considerably, in some cases to three or four times the normal figure.

According to official German statements, Luxemburg is subject to the same rationing scheme as Germany (since September 1940), but information from Luxemburg shows that the similarity exists more on paper than in reality, full rations not always being available.

According to the latest reports received in London the situation may be summarised as follows :

Obtainable : Bread, potatoes, the standard meat rations.

Unobtainable : Coffee, tea, cocoa, butter, bacon, and luxury foodstuffs such as chocolate, confectionery, etc.

The fat ration is not fully available. Flour is extracted at 91 per cent.

For table of the nominal rations see Appendix.

Clothing and Bedding

All textile fabrics and clothes are rationed and only obtainable against coupons. The number of coupons required is the same as in Germany and only little below the ration allowed in England, but whereas in England all coupons may be exchanged for goods, shops in Luxemburg are empty and cloth is almost unobtainable. Such cloth as is obtainable is of so a bad quality and so largely made of wood that it is hardly worth while buying. The same applies to bedding material, of which only insufficient quantities of very inferior quality can be had. Leather soles for shoes are not now to be had, wooden soles being mostly used.

The shortage of clothing materials is emphasised by the regular visits made by agents of the Winter Relief Fund. They compel people to open their wardrobes and chests-of-drawers and demand whatever they consider superfluous for the owners, especially woollen articles, blankets, fur coats, and so on.

Soap

One cake per person per month is the ration allowed, but it is said to be a mixture of soap and sand. In view of the harmful effects on the skin, special soap coupons are issued for small children.

Fuel

Fuel supplies are fairly good, and there was sufficient coal obtainable to avoid severe hardship during the winter months.

Medical Supplies

Two-thirds of all existing chemists had to close down owing to shortage of medical supplies. Aspirin and other essential drugs are scarce and are only obtainable on a physician's prescription.

II. EFFECTS OF WAR CONDITIONS ON CHILDREN

Nutrition, Health and Growth

At the beginning of the war the general standard of health among the child-population was very high. The authorities in the industrial districts of the South and of

Luxemburg-City had made considerable efforts to ensure
maximum care for school children ; medical supervision,
free school meals, shower baths, physical training,
collective trips, etc., were considered an essential part
of the physical and moral development of the child. No
doubt undernourishment is beginning to affect the
children's health, but it is believed that in the Grand
Duchy children are able to stand the present reduced
diet comparatively well, having laid in large stores of
vitality in the past. Furthermore, Luxemburg, not
being considered as occupied territory but as part of
Germany, has better food rations than its neighbours,
France and Belgium. Precise figures are not available
but the standard of health conforms more to the German
level than to that of France or Belgium.

Little information has been received as to any increase
in specified diseases.

Vital Statistics

Figures are not available. It is known, however, that
the German conception of sexual morality has disastrous
effects on young people and that the birth rate of
illegitimate children is higher than before (177 in 1936
or 3·27 per cent. of all births). On January 25, 1942,
no less than 25 Luxemburg girls of 13 to 17 years, were
at the Strasburg Maternity Hospital awaiting the birth
of their children, after having been raped by Germans.
(See also Family Life, p. 65.)

Education

Since the introduction of German Civil Administration
on August 7, 1940, substantial changes in education have
been imposed. To get a true picture of the present
situation, a few words must be said about the educational
system prior to the invasion.

Owing to the geographical situation of the Grand
Duchy, placed at the cross-roads where French and
German cultures meet, education in Luxemburg had a
bi-lingual and therefore special character. Laws were
promulgated in both languages, both of which were
official, though in general neither French nor German
was spoken in the home but a dialect peculiar to
Luxemburg. This dialect is basically German, but

so full of French and Celtic words and phrases that it is not easily comprehensible to Germans.

In the schools, German, from the first year, and French, from the second year, were taught and used for instruction.

One of the first changes made by the invaders was to forbid all use of French, though for 500 years it had been one of the official languages of Luxemburg. The Germans even prohibited all French expressions used in the Luxemburg dialect such as ' Madame ', ' merci', ' bonjour', etc. They punished with fines and even imprisonment the use of French accents in names. French names and surnames had to disappear in favour of German forms. Naturally, the bilingual school system was also abolished as was everything that might perpetuate French culture, loved and admired in Luxemburg. All existing text-books were confiscated and replaced by German books. All religious instruction was forbidden and priests were dismissed, deported into Germany or taken to concentration camps.* A great many members of the teaching profession were also dismissed and deported to Germany. German teachers have immigrated into Luxemburg, in many cases with their families, and are set to indoctrinate the children of the Grand Duchy with National-Socialist theories. Two out of the three secondary schools for boys (gymnasia) have been closed and very little time is spent on cultural education, the main duty of the German teacher being to make of the young Luxemburger an ardent German National-Socialist. According to information received by Luxemburg Government circles in London, the standard of the teaching staff imported from Germany is, as might be expected, inferior to the average Luxemburg teacher of pre-war days. In fact, it is no exaggeration to say that the very principles of traditional Luxemburg education have been repudiated.

From May to October 1940, this period including the summer holidays, the schools were closed, part of the population having been evacuated to France and the other part having moved from the south of the country to the north at that time. Since then, no interruption

---

* About 98 per cent. of the population is Roman Catholic, as were all elementary, and many secondary schools and colleges.

ın tho programmoo has oocurrod, the number of rohool periods and the size of classes being normal.

Family Life

As mentioned above, many people have been forced to take up work in Germany with the consequent breaking up of their homes.

All boys are compulsorily incorporated in the Hitler Youth and all girls in the Bund Deütscher Mädchen. The Germans are systematically trying to estrange children from their parents and denunciation is taught and favoured, as in the Reich.

Labour service is compulsory for all boys and girls of 18 years of age. In an address to one contingent of young girls leaving for a labour camp, the Chief of the German Civil Administration, Gauleiter Gustav Simon, said : ' You will be pleased that you are allowed to serve for six months in a German labour camp and proud to know that you may have the honour to return from there as German mothers'. In these camps, which are in the neighbourhood of soldiers' and men's labour-camps, the Luxemburg girls have to share dormitories with German girls, most of whom are expectant mothers and who proudly display a distinguishing armlet with the letters I.B.B.—' ich bin befruchtet ' (I am pregnant).

' In fact', writes Mr. Georges Schommer in a Memorandum on Post-War Youth Problems elaborated for the Luxemburg Government at the end of 1941, ' the régime encourages procreation in every possible way. This tendency appears clearly throughout the whole organisation of spare-time activities for youth and in the facilities there offered to satisfy the carnal instincts'.

Information has been received through a private report that, before leaving for the so-called labour camps, all young girls are medically examined and if they are unfortunate enough to be found sterile or if they are known to belong to an anti-German family, they are sent to German soldiers' brothels.

Behaviour and Social Adjustment

Nothing is known about young children. There appears to be considerable unrest among young people from

E

15 years upwards, and a great many arrests and convictions are reported for insults to the new régime and its agents, and for listening to and spreading B.B.C. news.

Juvenile Employment

All children over 12 years of age are incorporated in the German Labour Front and may at any moment be called up for agricultural work.

Recreation and Youth Organisations

All former youth organisations, including the Scout movement, have been dissolved and their assets and property confiscated. All sports organisations have been taken over and are now more concerned with preparation for military training than with athletics.

III. AMELIORATIVE MEASURES

All pre-war welfare organisations have been abolished and replaced by German social institutions, of which the most important is the Winter Relief Fund already mentioned.

The Luxemburg League of Patriots, an underground organisation founded to organise and encourage Luxemburg resistance to Germany, is known to give assistance and moral support to those people who have to suffer severely under German treatment.

Post-War Plans

The main concern of Luxemburg circles in Great Britain is the education or re-education of the young. This is the object of the Memorandum drawn up by Mr. Georges Schommer and already quoted on page 65. He shows that the whole German policy as regards Luxemburg youth is to replace all national traditions by the National-Socialist ideology, which, as is well known, is characterised by the principle that individualism is dangerous and that the child belongs to the community of which the State is the final expression. To render youth more receptive of that ideology everything is done to give rein to the carnal instincts and natural leanings of these inexperienced young people. Hence the tendency to eliminate as completely as possible the influence of the home, as well as its religious and moral influences. Hence also the extreme simplification of teaching, which

is confined mainly to German, singing, and physical
training. There are, too, other baits and attractions :
uniforms, games, living in common, the false camaraderie
of elders who mingle with the younger ones and share
their kind of life, early sexual emancipation, travel,
camping, etc.

In view of this systematic demoralisation of youth it
will not be enough to reinstate the pre-war educational
system. The scope and powers of the Department of
Public Instruction must be enlarged, it must become a
Department of National Education or even a Ministry
of Youth. The content of education will also have to
be revised, new teachers trained, new text-books printed.
At least as many facilities for recreational activities must
be given as under the Germans. The Scout Movement
will probably be the most appropriate form, since it is
inspired by principles of collaboration, solidarity,
moderation, and balance.

THE NETHERLANDS

I. GENERAL CONDITIONS

Up to the present, German policy in the Netherlands
has been dictated by the hope that the Dutch could be
induced to co-operate of their free will, rather than by
force. Hence, unlike some other occupied countries,
Holland has kept its central, provincial and local
government machinery, though the officials work under
the control of German Civil Commissioners. At the head
of this superimposed German Civil Administration is the
Civil Commissioner Seyss-Inquart, assisted by four
Directors of Departments—Public Security, Economy and
Finance, Administration and Justice, and Propaganda.

Population

The population of the Netherlands on December 31,
1937, was estimated to be 8,639,600, including about
120,000 Jews, most of whom were then living in
Amsterdam.

Children under 15 numbered 2,472,800 or 28·6 per cent.
of the total.

Economic Situation

The whole economic machinery has been adapted to the requirements of Germany, which has established a stranglehold over Dutch finance by the following methods : goods exported to Germany are paid for in German marks, but the Netherlands Bank is obliged to accept these marks and pay the exporter in guilders at a rate of exchange fixed by Germany. Similarly, the bank has to pay in guilders to the families of Dutch people working in Germany the money remitted by the workers in marks, and also the interest on German securities owned by Dutch people. As a consequence, the German nominal debt to the Netherlands Bank mounts steadily ; on May 25, 1942, it was 1,298 million guilders. Prior to April 1, 1941, the Dutch-German clearing was financed by the Dutch Treasury, but on that date the clearing system was abolished. The Dutch Treasury has to meet the cost of German occupation, estimated at a hundred million guilders a month. The National Debt has risen, as a result, from four milliards of guilders to seven milliards in two years of occupation. The Netherlands, therefore, is not in a position to buy goods against those it sells ; there is a one-way traffic of goods and services, offset only by a huge accumulating debt. The impoverishment of the country and a steady deterioration in the once high standard of living is an obvious result.

(i) *Agriculture*

By a German decree 50 per cent. of all fresh vegetables must be exported to Germany, and 80 per cent. of tomatoes and cucumbers. Manufacturers of tinned and preserved vegetables may sell only for export.

On October 16, 1941, the *Deutsche Allgemeine Zeitung* stated : ' One of the most important suppliers of the German market is Holland, which today sends roughly 70 per cent. of its harvest to Germany.' The *Wirtschaftsdienst*, November 7, 1941, said that German wheat requirements exceeded the Dutch capacity to export and it was hoped that this state of affairs would be remedied by the ploughing programme for 1942.

This ploughing programme, the lack of imported fodder and the shortage of fertilizers has resulted in a great reduction of livestock. It was reported by the *Haagsche Post* on March 1, 1941, that 60 per cent. of the country's pigs had been slaughtered. Milch cows were reduced from $1\frac{1}{2}$ million to $1\frac{1}{4}$ million in 1940–41 (*Kölnische Zeitung,* March 13, 1941) and the milk production for the year 1941–42 was estimated by the Dutch Agricultural Institute of Economics to be 30 per cent. below that of 1939–40. (*De Telegraaf,* May 16, 1941.)

(ii) *Industry*

Dutch industry is handicapped by the shortage of raw materials ; only such firms as are working to German orders receiving supplies.

The registered unemployed, who numbered 300,000 before the occupation, were about 100,000 during the winter of 1941–42, but about 200,000 men are working in Germany (Zeesen Radio, March 26, 1942) and the number of unemployed who do not register for fear of being sent to Germany is believed to be fairly high.

All Jewish businesses (20,000) have been taken over by German overseers and, in many cases, liquidated.

Food

It is estimated that the standard ration plus an estimate for unrationed foodstuffs allow for the following amounts of calories as compared before the war.

	Average per head of population before the war	NORMAL CONSUMERS			
		Jan. 1941	May 1941	Jan. 1942	June 1942
Rationed foodstuffs	2,464	2,216	1,940	1,640	1,386
Unrationed ,,	300	200	200	120	100
	2,764	2,416	2,140	1,760	1,486

As a rule only butter is available. Last year households with incomes below 1,400 florins (£175) got a price reduction of 0·90 florins on kilogrammes of butter. This allowance is no longer given so that it is unlikely that these consumers who have to pay now 2·60 florins per kilogramme (about 3s. per lb) for their fat ration, are able to buy this ration fully.

Fish is not rationed but there is hardly any available, war conditions having all but put a stop to sea-fishing.

In addition to the heavy export of food, Holland has to feed worn-out troops sent to her country for recuperation, as well as large numbers of German officials, women and children. Ration cards held by members of the German armed forces must be given precedence over all others. (*Deutsche Zeitung in den Niederlanden*, January 16, 1941.)

For table of weekly rations see Appendix.

Clothing

Clothing is rationed at 120 points per year. The sale of socks, stockings and underwear is very restricted. Leather shoes are nearly unobtainable. For a new winter coat, which requires 80 points, a special permit is required. Prices are such that those with small incomes cannot afford to buy new clothes. Household linen, sewing material and darning wool are included in the rationing scheme. No pure wool is obtainable and various substitutes are being used or tried. Second-hand clothing can be sold at half the point value of similar new articles.

On December 29, 1941, an announcement was issued by the Secretary-General of the Ministry of Trade, Industry, and Shipping, to the effect that all stocks of woollen and fur goods belonging to manufacturers, wholesalers or retailers, must be reported to the Reich Textile Bureau at the Hague. On the following day it was announced that the sale of these goods had been blocked and they must be put at the disposal of the Hague Government Office (Distex). The regulations were extended later to leather clothes. (*Standard*, December 30, 1941.)

Fuel

Coal is strictly rationed and people get only a fraction of the amount they used before. Few, if any, households can heat more than one room very moderately.

Gas and electricity have been rationed since December 1940. On July 1, 1941, consumption was limited to 75 per cent. of the amount consumed in the corresponding period of 1940 ; in addition ' gas-less ' hours at certain times of day were introduced in Amsterdam, Rotterdam and the Hague, and it was announced that those who

exceeded their ration would have their supply cut off,
a threat which in some cases was later carried out.

Medical Supplies

There is an increasing shortage of medicines and
bandages are very scarce (*Limburgisch Dagblad*, February
2, 1942). The *Haagsche Courant* reported on April 27,
1942, that no toothbrushes had been available anywhere
for weeks.

II. EFFECTS OF WAR CONDITIONS ON CHILDREN

Health and Diseases

We have very little precise information, but the following facts have been reported : Families of every category,
rich as well as poor, are affected with head-lice ; diphtheria
was prevalent in West Brabant throughout the winter
of 1941–42 and schools had to be closed.

Vital Statistics

There was a slight increase in the birth rate in 1940,
from 20·5 per thousand in 1938 to 20·9 in 1940.   The
increase in the death rate (not including death by enemy
action) was, however, much more marked.

Death rate per thousand :	1939	1940	1941
Under 1 year	100	118	130
1 to 4 years	100	115	134
5 to 14 years	100	110	127
15 to 24 years	100	106	143
General death rate	100	109	117

It is expected that the death rate for 1942 will be even
higher, in view of the deterioration of the food situation.

Education

Although a few school buildings have been requisitioned,
schooling seems to be affected mostly in the political
sense.   For instance, 200 young Dutch teachers were
sent to Oldenburg to study the German educational
system (*Olderburgische Staatszeitung*, February 27, 1941) ;
the number of hours devoted to the teaching of German
in secondary schools has been increased at the expense
of French and English (*Handelsblad*, June 30, 1941), and
sentences have been deleted from text-books.

About 70 per cent. of the elementary schools in Holland are free schools, receiving financial support from the State, but with the right of appointing teachers in accordance with the principles of the school. The Secretary-General of the Department of Education decreed however that, whenever a new teacher had to be nominated, the school board must submit to him a recommendation of three persons, of whom he might eliminate one or more. If no trustworthy person were recommended he reserved the right to nominate one himself. This decree raised a storm of protests and by March 1, 1942, 1,271 school-boards out of 1,500 had written to the Department that they refused to co-operate on such a basis.*

A circular of the same Department complains that many parents have applied to have their children transferred to other schools on personal or political grounds ; such a transfer will be granted only if parents can produce the written permission of the head of the original school. (*Leidsche Dagblad*, March 4, 1942.) The Chief Inspector for Education in Gelderland, Brabant and Limburg, Vlekke, stated in an interview with *Volk on Vaderland* (Rotterdam, April 20, 1942) that, since children were interested in politics, if a teacher did not understand the new conditions in Europe he would pass on this misunderstanding to his pupils. (Teachers repeatedly compare the period from 1795 to 1813 with the present one.) He pointed out to 17 inspectors that if they were aware of this attitude on the part of the teachers and did not take measures against it, he would ask for their dismissal. Only one inspector, he said, understood his views ; the others replied that they were sincere Roman Catholics and would never do anything against their convictions. The popularity of the Roman Catholic schools, which exist mainly in the south of the country, has been increasing. However, on February 23, 1941, Professor Van Dam, the Nazi Secretary-General of the Ministry of Education, Science, and Culture, announced that the salaries of all teachers who were members of religious orders would be cut by 40 per cent., and that all

* *The Times Educational Supplement*, May 23, 1942.

headmasters who were also priests would be forced to resign. (*Vrij Nederland*, March 1, 1941.)

On the other hand a great many new German schools have been opened all over the country.

The matriculation examination for 1942 has had to be simplified, especially in science and mathematics, and one of the reasons given is that homework cannot be done adequately when only one room in the house is heated and has to be used for all purposes. Moreover, the children's capacity for study is lowered by poor diet. (*De Telegraaf*, November 2, 1941.)

Behaviour and Juvenile Delinquency

Juvenile delinquency is reported to have increased throughout the country, especially at Rotterdam 'as a result of the suffering caused by the war '.* (*Nieuwe Rotterdamsche Courant*, March 1, 1942.)

At Amsterdam cases of theft by juveniles have increased from 1880 in January 1940, to 3,551 (including 917 bicycle thefts) in January 1942, but during the same period offences against public morality have decreased by eight. Local authorities have, however, established a curfew for young girls unaccompanied by a parent or guardian ; at Maestricht no girl under 18 can be out of doors from a half hour after sunset and no girl under age can go to a café after 7 p.m. (*Het Nationale Dagblad*, March 11, 1942.)   At Leyden, Utrecht, Rotterdam, and Velsen, no unaccompanied girl under 16 may be at a place of entertainment after 6 p.m. (*De Telegraaf*, February 26, 1942.)

A Rotterdam Justice of the Peace, who imposed fines on school-children for attacking National Socialist Movement children, ruled that juvenile crime should be dealt with by a Juvenile Court only if it were not of a political character. (*De Telegraaf*, November 2, 1941.)

Youth Organisations

The Dutch Boy Scouts have been disbanded by order of Seyss-Inquart on the grounds that the organisation has been ' an instrument of English influence '. (*Reuter*,

---

* 25,000 houses were destroyed during the bombing attack on May 14, 1940.

April 4, 1941.) The German police at Putten used weapons against Boy Scouts who ' resisted and insulted them'; one boy aged 16 was severely injured. (*Deutsche Zeitung*, July 29, 1941.)

The National-Socialist Youth Movement has now a membership of 15,000 Dutch boys and girls under 18. (*Nieuweblad van het Norden*, Groningen, March 25, 1942.)

A branch of the Hitler Youth has been established in the Netherlands for children who have at least one German parent.

III. AMELIORATIVE MEASURES

Pre-War Health and Welfare Services

In general these function very much along their former lines, although under German control, and they have retained their pre-war staffs.

German military authorities have taken over many hospitals and sanatoria, so that tuberculosis patients can no longer be properly isolated and treated. (Private report, May 1942.)

De Tjid of March 3, 1942, gives the following indications as to recipients of Poor Relief :

	October 1941	February 1942
Families ..	56,893	64,435
Single persons ..	30,425	30,769
	1940	1941
Sums disbursed ..	40,120,000 guilders	41,304,000 guilders

War Relief

The Government Bureau for Food Supply in War-time plans to distribute vitamin C tablets gratis to certain groups of the population.   Pupils in infant and elementary schools are to have three tablets (50 mg. each) per week for nine weeks.   Expectant mothers will receive 50 tablets. (*Allgemeen Handelsblad*, May 15, 1942.)

School meals are organised by local authorities—for instance at Dordrecht, where children will get five warm meals a week.   The meals will be the same as those served in public kitchens, they will be coupon-free and parents are expected to pay according to their means. (*Deutsche Zeitung in den Niederlanden*, April 13, 1942.)

Small groups of children have occasionally been invited to Germany for a few weeks to recuperate.

NORWAY*

I. GENERAL CONDITIONS

The total population of Norway did not quite reach three millions in 1938, with about 57,000 more women than men.   Children under 15 numbered 674,503, of whom 387,308 were of school age (7–14).

Present Economic Situation

As in all occupied territories, there is in Norway an acute shortage of goods and a swelling volume of currency and credit.   The upward movement of the price level has to some extent been checked by a rigid price-control system, extensive rationing of the goods still available and a far-reaching control of wages and incomes.

Nominal wages, with some exceptions, have remained the same, with the result that real wages, it was estimated in May 1942, have decreased by about 30 per cent.

Although industry is handicapped by lack of raw materials, available statistics show that there is no unemployment since labour exchanges can hardly find enough workers for the timber industry or to man the extensive building programme of fortifications, roads, etc. Many unemployed men, however, object to working in the interests of the Germans and do not register.   They do not therefore, draw unemployment allowances, but they are helped secretly by their fellow countrymen, thanks to the extraordinary national solidarity which prevails.   There are naturally no figures for these unregistered unemployed.   A few thousand workers have been moved from one part of the country to another, but only a few hundreds, out of the 20,000 that were asked for, have volunteered for work in Germany itself. According to recent information (June 1942) compulsory labour will be extended to large groups of the population.

---

* Most of the information concerning Norway has kindly been supplied by the following Norwegian officials : Mr. Knut Getz Wold, of the Ministry of Finance, Dr. A. Sommerfelt, of the Ministry of Education, Mr. John Caspersen, Deputy Director of Norwegian Public Health Services, and Mr. Njaa, of the Ministry of Social Welfare.

Movements of Population

A great part of the population fled from the fighting areas during the hostilities, but returned home almost immediately after and thus never became a serious problem. The civilian population of part of the coast was compulsorily evacuated by the German military authorities. It is believed that, helped by the national solidarity already mentioned, they have settled, as best as they could, in other parts of the country, but there is no definite information on this point.

Inadequate housing and the consequent overcrowding have created a serious problem in towns such as Bodö, Molde, etc., which suffered badly from air-raids and bombardment.

Food

Fishing, once a great national industry and source of revenue, is handicapped through lack of shipping, lack of fuel oil, mines and other war conditions, so that fish, even for home consumption, is rather scarce. The once prosperous dairy industry is suffering because a large proportion of the cattle has had to be slaughtered for lack of imported fodder. Stocks of foodstuffs, which had been accumulated in the country, have been requisitioned and exported to Germany, as well as a large proportion of the fish still caught, and of meat and dairy products. Wheat had always to be imported as the home crop was far from sufficient (in 1937, 203,675 metric tons of wheat was imported against 53,937 tons home-produced). The difficulties of inland transport and the insufficiency of coastal shipping, as well as the feeding of the Army of Occupation and other Germans (such as some thousand pregnant German women for whom large quantities of milk and other dairy products are reserved) are additional reasons for the shortage of food in cities. People in the country are, naturally, better off for food, and a large proportion of city-dwellers have friends and relatives in the country who give them various foodstuffs or surreptitiously sell to them at reasonable prices.

In considering the weekly rations (see table in Appendix) it must be remembered that fish bulked largely in the pre-war Norwegian diet, as did milk, butter and cheese.

Moreover, few vegetables and little fruit can be grown in the central and northern parts of the country, and importation of citrus fruit, which was very considerable in peace time, has now completely stopped. Until recently potatoes seem to have been the main item of the war diet. It is not always possible, particularly in outlying districts, to obtain the full allowance of rationed foods. People who escaped to Sweden in the spring of 1942 reported a growing scarcity of all foods, including those which are rationed. In February the fat ration amounted to only 25-30 grammes a day or the equivalent of the lowest ration in Germany during the World War, and the situation was worse in March when, through lack of raw materials, there was no margarine. About 55,000 tons of vegetable, fish and whale oil were used in the manufacture of margarine before the war; now at most 10,000 tons are available for this purpose.

Potatoes completely disappeared from the city markets in the spring of 1942; the prospects for the 1942 crops are, however, regarded as very good. The supply of fresh vegetables was stated to be fairly good in June.

Meat is very scarce in cities, where the amount available rarely exceeds 200 grammes a month, instead of the nominal ration of 100 grammes per week.

Clothing and Bedding

Clothing is rationed on the points system. The number of points is, however, inadequate to cover the needs of growing children. The cards for children between 5 and 16 years, issued for a period of 15 months, contain 240 points. Here are the points required for various articles for girls : woollen dress 70 points, winter coat 150, summer woollen coat 110, cotton summer frock 75, etc. It is generally possible to obtain these.

For infants a special application has to be made in each case and supplies are now very scarce.

Shoes are almost impossible to get, such leather as remains in the country being used for German military supplies. The *Stockholms Tidningen* announced on February 7, 1942, that paper shoes with birch soles would soon be available.

Woollen blankets (one per family) and warm clothing were requisitioned in November 1941.

Soap

The monthly ration of soap is 125 grammes (4½ ozs.) of the so-called ' B ' soap, which is of inferior quality and 250 grammes (9 ozs.) of soap powder. Medicated soap for skin diseases is obtainable only on a doctor's prescription.

Fuel

Coal and coke are no longer available for household use. The supply of wood has been greatly increased, but it is not always easy to get in cities on account of transport difficulties. The price index for fuel is about two and a half times the pre-war level.

Medical Supplies

In anticipation of a possible blockade, both the Government and the wholesale firms had built up large reserves of emergency supplies, but these are now becoming exhausted, especially in the case of medicaments not manufactured in the country, which it is now impossible to import. The sale of certain medical supplies has had to be restricted, and it is particularly difficult to obtain the fat ingredients needed as a foundation for ointments, sulphatiasole and similar preparations, as well as those containing vitamins. Stocks of cod-liver oil were very large at the outbreak of war, and the chemists introduced a kind of voluntary rationing so that it can still be had. Formerly some insulin was manufactured in the country and some imported from Denmark and other countries ; now the supply is much reduced. These difficulties are further aggravated in some regions, especially in the north, by poor communications.

II. EFFECTS OF WAR CONDITIONS ON CHILDREN

Nutrition, Health and Growth

If rations were ample at the outbreak of war, they were soon reduced, so that it was to be expected that the health of the population would suffer accordingly, the more so as the housing situation, the lack of fuel, of soap and hot water, and other accompaniments of war all have their effects.

There are, however, no figures available and no comprehensive report has reached Great Britain so far. It seems that the previous fairly high standard of life—with consequent ' family stocks '—and the help given to the less fortunate members of the community by the more fortunate have counterbalanced, for a few months at least, the effects of the food shortage.

Loss of weight both among adults and children is reported generally and from some places there are reports of hypoavitaminosis (vitamin starvation).

Diseases

Epidemiological diseases—scarlet fever, measles and chicken pox—greatly increased in 1941. There were then more cases of diphtheria than for any other year since the last war. Tuberculosis, which had been decreasing during past years, followed the downward trend until the beginning of 1941 ; the curve then started rising in the second half of that year. Specialists expect a further increase in 1942. Impetigo contagiosa and scabies are also on the increase, as well as syphilis and gonorrhœa. There is a good deal of trouble of the digestive organs and much catarrhal disease.

Vital Statistics

The birth rate, which was 15·55 in 1938 and 15·9 in 1939, actually increased to 16·3 in 1940, because the emotional conditions due to the outbreak of the war brought about many new unions. It has decreased again, but there is otherwise very little information available.

Education

The schooling of children has been seriously affected by the war.

Schools were closed during hostilities and only a limited number could be reopened afterwards, either because the buildings had been destroyed by fire or bombing, or because they had been requisitioned to serve as barracks or hospitals for the Army of Occupation. This has affected school hours and probably also the size of classes.

In Oslo, for instance, where most of the former school buildings are not available, some of the children have to be taught in the morning and the others in the afternoon. In some places they are even taught in three shifts.

The difficulty of providing fuel has led to the Christmas holidays being prolonged and the summer ones shortened.

Many schools, elementary, secondary, and vocational, have been closed for longer or shorter periods in reprisal for the patriotic attitude and activities of the pupils ; headmasters and teachers have been dismissed. There is a good deal of tension in every type of school owing to the activities of the Hird, the Quisling Youth Movement. Its members are instructed to act as informers, and clashes have occurred, resulting in pupils being beaten and maltreated. Pupils have been expelled and forbidden admission in other schools until they can prove six months' ' good conduct'. In many cases, private instruction has been arranged for expelled children.

Matters came to a head in February 1942, when two new measures were taken by the authorities : the first compelled all teachers to join the newly-formed Teachers' Front, under penalty of being dismissed from their posts without pay or pension, and becoming liable to be recruited for ' useful work ' in north Norway and elsewhere ; the second decreed the compulsory enrolment of all children between 10 and 18 in the National-Socialist Youth Movement. At the same time, new regulations regarding school discipline and teaching methods were issued by the Ministry for Church and Education : Quisling's portrait was to be displayed in all schools ; at least one half-hour weekly was to be devoted to instruction on the doctrines of the National-Socialist Party ; children who showed disrespect for teachers or fellow pupils who are members of the Nasjonal Samling were to be expelled and even sent to reformatories.

This resulted in a vigorous protest from the teachers. Out of 14,000, over 12,000 sent to the Ministry letters resigning from the Teachers' Front, protesting against the regimentation of the school children, and stating they were unable to co-operate in the conduct of education along the lines demanded by the Nasjonal Samling. The teachers' protest was backed by local school authorities and by parents all over the country, as well as by the Church.

The Ministry invited teachers to reconsider their decision under threat of compulsory manual labour and closed the schools throughout Norway for one month because of ' fuel shortage'. The teachers remained firm although many hundreds of them have been arrested (1,300 at the end of March) and sent to the Grini concentration camp or to forced labour, along with Russian prisoners of war. In the second half of April a further 500 were sent to compulsory labour in the North. These were followed shortly afterwards by another batch of 110, and nothing has been heard of their ultimate fate.

The Easter holiday followed the ' fuel holiday', and schools were due to re-open on April 9. On April 8, the Ministry announced that no teacher would be forced to join the Teachers' Front, but that all teachers who resumed their duties in the schools would be considered *ipso facto* members, while those who refused to sign an acknowledgment of their membership would receive no salary. On the next day, in all the schools where work was resumed, the teachers read out a declaration maintaining their protest against membership of the Teachers' Front and their intention out of loyalty to their calling to continue to teach in accordance with the wishes of the pupils and their parents.

Only a limited number of schools was re-opened (one with 250 pupils in the whole of Oslo), because so many teachers had been arrested and a number of school buildings had been put to other uses in the meantime. In addition, schools can be closed—or remain closed—if the local Agricultural Committee and Labour Exchange declare that the work of the children and their teachers is required on farms.

Attempts to train new teachers by a short course have failed, because too few candidates came forward. On April 15, the Oslo radio station announced that all Teachers' Training Schools would be closed until further notice.

Changes of curriculum have not yet been very considerable. It has been decided that in elementary schools, German should take the place of English. In the gymnasia, the ' English line ' is to be replaced by a ' German line'. New text-books, particularly history text-books, are being prepared.

Family Life

Except in cases where some member of the family belongs to the Quisling Party, present conditions have knit the family closer together, both in a spiritual and in a material sense, because relatives, whose homes had been destroyed, have been given hospitality. The noble solidarity which can be observed throughout the country finds its first expression in the family circles.

Although military prisoners were released immediately on the cessation of hostilities, a good many families are still dispersed. Such is the case with the families of political prisoners, whose number is unknown; of those whose breadwinner has been forcibly transferred to work in some other part of the country ; and above all of those of which some member is abroad with the Mercantile Marine or the Free Forces. Sailors' families are accustomed to a certain amount of separation, but in present circumstances that separation is much longer and much more drastic, and it involves greater material and emotional suffering on the part of those who are left behind.

Dependency

There seems to be no ground for assuming that the number of orphaned, abandoned, or neglected children has increased as a result of the war. There were only about 1,450 men killed during hostilities, mostly young and unmarried, so that the number of war orphans is probably quite small. They are, as a rule, provided for by their own relatives with the financial help of the State.

According to two official Decrees issued on December 9, 1941, a yearly pension of 1,200 kroner is granted—with additional allowances for children—to widows of soldiers killed in action, and of men serving in the auxiliary military organisations. Similar, but slightly reduced, pensions are given to dependants of seamen, fishermen and other civilian war victims.

About 7,000 people are known to have been arrested, sometimes both the husband and the wife, and a few hundreds have been shot.

A special section has been set up at the Grini concentration camp for children (from four years upwards) whose parents are opposing the present régime, either in the country or abroad.

Behaviour and Social Adjustment

There are no reliable statistics. It is, however, known that the active part taken by children and young people in resistence to the invader makes them far more independent and increases their sense of responsibility. They are deeply impressed by the fight put up by their teachers, and even elementary school children have demonstrated against the Quisling régime, have suffered arrest, and have been sent to reformatories.

It is reported that the director of one reformatory has been dismissed because he refused to keep in his institution some boys who had been sent there for political reasons and who, he maintained, were in no need of re-education.

The national struggle absorbs so much of the interest, attention and power of concentration of the young, that it is said to be very difficult to keep their attention on study and education. Every possibility of controlling the environment of young people having disappeared, the task of preparing them for their future social duties and responsibilities becomes very difficult.

Juvenile Employment

No information available, except as indicated under 'Education,' *supra*.

Recreation and Youth Organisations

All youth organisations have been dissolved and, as mentioned above, enrolment in the Nasjonal Samling Youth Movement has been made compulsory for all children and young people between 10 and 18, since February 1942, but it has not yet been enforced, in view of the strong opposition of the teachers, the Church, the parents, and the children themselves.

According to a speech by the leader of the Movement, Axel Stang, all members may be summoned for compulsory physical training and labour service during their free time.

It is difficult to give the young any wholesome recreation, even privately. Food restrictions and fuel shortage prevent any social or family gatherings; all communal arrangements are impossible and dancing is prohibited; tours and excursions are made more difficult by the black-out and the food and travel restrictions.

III. AMELIORATIVE MEASURES

Survival of Pre-War Services

The administration of health and social services was first conducted along pre-war lines but, since the beginning of 1942, reorganisation is taking place along National Socialist lines and ' racial ' discrimination is prescribed. This is partly opposed by local authorities, with consequent confusion and insecurity.

The value of the payments in cash provided under the various schemes has, however, been greatly reduced during the Occupation because of the rise in the cost of living. Workers' and employers' contributions for unemployment insurance have been increased.

The efficiency of some services is reduced because, since they have been taken over by Quisling staffs, the population has lost confidence and does not make the same use of them ; this seems to be the case, in particular, with the maternity and child welfare centres, which used to be much used.

Certificates for butter, milk, cream, wheat, flour, and eggs are valid only if issued by doctors who are members of the new National-Socialist Medical Association. (*Nya Dagligt Allehanda*, February 20, 1942.)

Relief Measures

At the beginning of the war, the Nasjonalhjelpen, a national relief organisation with branches all over the country, was created. It did much good work until it was taken over by the Quislings in the autumn of 1941. Thanks to funds and gifts in kind collected in the country itself or sent from abroad, mostly from Sweden, it sought to provide food, clothes, housing and medical supplies for the families whose homes had been destroyed or who were otherwise in need as a result of the war. The Nasjonalhjelpen arranged meals in nearly every school and it ran a ' photocard ' scheme, out of which 13,800 children received 30 kroner a month.

Plans for Post-War Relief and Social Reconstruction

These are now under consideration by the Norwegian Government in Great Britain.

POLAND*

I. GENERAL CONDITIONS

In accordance with the German-Soviet agreement of September 28, 1939, the Republic of Poland was partitioned as follows :

(i) 72,866 square miles, with a population of some 22,250,000 were taken by Germany.

(ii) A territory of 77,260 square miles, with a population of some 13,090,000 came under Soviet occupation.

The Germans divided their share into two parts : the first, *i.e.* the western part with considerable portions of Central and Northern Poland (including the important towns of Poznan, Katowice, Bydgoszcz, Torun, Lodz, Ciechanow, etc.) with a population of about 10,700,000, was incorporated in the German Reich.

The second part, including the towns of Warsaw, Cracow, Tarnopol, Stanislawow and Przemysl, with a population of some 11,600,000 in 1939 (since 1940, about 19,000,000) became a ' General Government ' placed under the authority of the Reich.

The intention of the occupying power is completely to Germanise the part incorporated in the Reich. With this object, the whole Polish and Jewish population of this area (in 1939 it represented 93·5 per cent. of the total) is either being sent to forced labour in Germany (over 400,000) or being expelled to the General Government (over 1,200,000). These people are replaced by Germans, taken partly from Eastern Europe (the Baltic States,

---

* Most of the information was drawn from ' The New German Order in Poland,' published for the Polish Ministry of Information by Hutchinson, London, 1942, and from various other sources, supplied by Mme. Grabinska.

Bessarabia, the Dobroudja, etc.) and partly from the
Reich itself. The second part, while remaining a
' settlement for Poles ' is almost entirely administered by
Germans.

This report proposes to deal only with the General
Government and the areas incorporated in the Reich ;
too little being known of the part originally occupied by
the U.S.S.R., but now also under German rule.

On December 31, 1938, the total population of Poland
was 35,090,000, of whom 11,413,000, or 32·6 per cent.
were children under 15.

All the information concerning the Jewish population
is grouped in a separate chapter (page 105) as they are
subjected to a régime very different from that applied to
the Poles.

Present Economic Conditions

(i) *Agriculture.*—The areas incorporated in the Reich
and those taken by the U.S.S.R. in 1939 furnished
Central Poland with their excess of agricultural produce
since Central Poland was never self-supporting in this
respect, producing only about 40 per cent. of its own
requirements. Central Poland now forms the main
portion of the General Government and since, owing to
the forcible removal of Poles and Jews from the
incorporated portion, the density of population has
increased from 93 to 113 per square mile, the situation
is serious. The depredations of war and the system of
German requisitioning made the problem acute right
from the beginning of the occupation.

In the General Government each village has to furnish
a certain amount of its produce, but this is often fixed at
a rate in excess of actual production, so that peasants
and farmers either starve, or are sent to concentration
camps, accused of economic sabotage. In return for their
produce they are given certificates enabling them to buy
petrol, tobacco and spirits—spirits being sold at a very
low price. The penalties for non-delivery of the full
quota requisitioned are savage : seizure of all live-stock
and all possessions, even clothing, imprisonment of the
peasants and expulsion of their families from their homes,

(ii) *Industry and Cost of Living.*—Many factories were destroyed during the war ; of those remaining many have had their equipment confiscated, or else have to work to German orders. Wages are fixed by the occupying authorities, mostly at the pre-war rate, while taxes have been doubled and the cost of living has risen to a fantastic height. It is estimated by the Polish Government that if 100 be taken as the index figure for the summer of 1939, the cost of living had risen to 360 by September 1940, and to 1,212 by September 1941.

The following comparative tables of prices in Warsaw gives some idea of the increase :

		Pre-War	September 1940	September 1941
		zlotys	zlotys	zlotys
Bread	per kilogramme	0·26	1·62	6·77
Meat (beef)	,, ,,	1·58	7·03	19·21
Potatoes	,, ,,	0·12	0·34	2·20
Sugar	,, ,,	1·00	6·40	20·93
Coal	,, 10 kilogrammes	0·48	1·59	12·94

NOTE.—Before the war £1= 25 zlotys.

These figures are based on the prices of essential goods but, in fact, many of these goods are unobtainable save on the black market.

(iii) *Unemployment.*—In the whole of Poland there is widespread unemployment among all intellectual and clerical workers, who are forced to take up manual labour.

In the incorporated territory, a Decree of September 17, 1940, provides for confiscation of the property of people who had fled or who had been absent from their domicile for some time ; those who had been expelled being classed as absentees. All Jewish property was also seized as well as Polish property in so far as it was required by German interests or for the ' strengthening of Germanism'. As a result there is not a single Pole left in a responsible position in industry, agriculture or commerce. Farms, businesses, shops, factories of all kinds, are now being exploited by Germans brought from the Baltic States or from other out-lying German colonies.

Movements of Population

Movement of population has taken place on a larger scale in Poland than in any other occupied country,

During the war itself, hundreds of thousands of civilians moved eastwards only to retrace their steps when Russia attacked Poland on September 17, 1939, whilst a few thousands found their way across the frontiers to Rumania, Hungary and Lithuania.

Even larger groups of the population were forcibly moved by the German authorities after the cessation of hostilities, especially in connection with the Germanisation of the incorporated territory. The exact number of Poles thus transferred from the incorporated area to the General Government exceeds 1,200,000.* Many instances are given of the forcible evacuation from towns and villages of the majority of the Polish population (in some cases of all Polish inhabitants) and the brutal manner in which these evacuations were carried out. Many people died from cold, exposure and starvation in the winter of 1939–40, when most of these compulsory evacuations took place. They have not yet, however, ceased entirely.

Owing to lack of transport, people recently expelled from their homes in the Western Provinces are not transferred to the General Government, but left to find new habitations for themselves. They are unable to get social assistance of any kind and they often wander long distances without being able or permitted to settle. This leads to many being arrested as vagrants and even to some being executed by the German authorities as ' Volksschädling', *i.e.* as useless and dangerous persons.

Similar expulsions happen, though on a smaller scale in the General Government. In Warsaw, for example, about 80,000 Poles had to move out of the district marked as the ghetto, whilst 110,000 Jews had to move in within twelve days (by October 31, 1940).

Forced Labour

There are more than 1,500,000 Polish workers in the Reich, brought there from over the whole Polish territory, including 200,000 prisoners of war. In the German paper, *Reichsarbeitsblatt*, in December 1941, Dr. Timm, of the Ministry of Labour in Berlin, stated that as the volun-

---

* It is estimated that about 1,500,000 civilians, in addition to over 100,000 prisoners of war, were transported to Russia from the areas first occupied by that country.

tary enrolment of Poles to work in Germany did not produce the required amount of man-power the German administration had recourse to compulsion. The Poles represent actually about 25 per cent. of all foreign workers in Germany.

In 1942 (January to June) women and girls made up as much as half of the contingents of workers sent to Germany. This included a certain number of very young people since, as regards work, children from 12 years upwards, are treated as adults.

Food

In the General Government there are three different ration scales—those for Germans, for Poles and for Jews respectively. Germans get the same rations as in Germany, Poles get less than Germans, and Jews less than Poles.

Recent rationing regulations are not available and vary, in many cases, from place to place, and from week to week. In any case rations can never be obtained in full, for instance as regards milk only a fraction of the children entitled to it can obtain it.

Tables of the quantitites of standard rationed foods will be found in the Appendix. In reading them it should be borne in mind :

(a) That Poles have no right to wheaten bread, barley, flour, milk, butter, fruit, and the better kind of vegetables.

(b) That only Polish children under one can obtain whole milk ; children from one to two are entitled to skimmed milk but older children only if they have a medical certificate.

Children under two have no ration cards, probably in accordance with the confidential circular issued by Governor-General Frank on January 25, 1940, which states :

‘ In connection with the food supply for the population, at all costs the efficiency of those engaged on work of military or vital importance must be maintained, while the rest of the population must be reduced to a minimum of food during the shortage ’.

During the first half of 1941, the caloric value of the food allotted to Poles in Warsaw was only about 680 (for

Jews 400′ only) or a quarter of normal requirements. The amount of protein was only 10 per cent. to 15 per cent. of requirements and that of fats 1 per cent. to 2 per cent.

The private sale of food and the transport of food, even of small quantities, is punishable by death in both areas. Killing a pig or other animal on one's own farm without a permit is also punishable by death, and the German Press has published instances of several such sentences being carried out.

From the Incorporated Area less information is available but rations are certainly not larger than in the General Government.

Not only are rations for Poles much less than those for Germans, but Poles are not admitted to the markets before 11 a.m. nor to the shops before noon, so that foodstuffs are often sold out before Poles are able to start their shopping. As a general rule, Germans have to be served first at all times.

Clothing

Clothing ration cards are not given out automatically ; they must be applied for and are not always granted. As there is, however, practically nothing in the shops to buy many people do not trouble to apply for the cards.

The amount available for sale during the past year was no more than one dress or suit for one person in twenty and one article of underwear for one person in three.

The impossibility of getting any new clothing bears hardly on the poorer people who have no reserves, and on those who have had to leave their homes at short notice with only a very limited amount of luggage. The lack of material obliges some Polish mothers, it is reported, to use newspapers to wrap their babies in. Peasants are not entitled to any clothing cards at all. They can only get clothes second-hand at exorbitant prices, so they are mostly in rags and have often to go without shoes, even in winter.

Soap

Very scarce. In Warsaw none has been available since April 1940.

Fuel

Since the winter of 1939–40, fuel has been extremely scarce, owing mainly to lack of supplies, though partly also to lack of transport. In Warsaw, in 1939, the situation was the more serious because of the fact that window panes, broken in large numbers during the siege, had not been repaired. This has since been made good, but the supply of fuel seems to have been no more adequate during the winters of 1940–41 and 1941–42. In the winter of 1941–42 it was extremely difficult to get any coal or wood, even on the black market. Families had not only to give up all hope of heating their homes, but, owing to a further restriction on the consumption of electricity, they experienced great difficulty even in cooking their meals.

Medical Supplies and Facilities

After the occupation, all medical supplies and the most modern hospital equipment were immediately requisitioned by the German authorities and very little has been imported since.

Many hospitals and tuberculosis sanatoria, some of which had very up-to-date equipment, were reserved for the exclusive use of Germans. In other hospitals, only a few wards are set aside for Poles and, as a result, there is very serious overcrowding. Instances are cited of maternity hospitals where 30 to 40 women are crowded in wards planned for eight beds. Polish women may remain only three days in hospital whilst German mothers are allowed eight days after the birth of the child. As a consequence most Polish confinements now take place at home, sometimes in very insanitary conditions, in consequence of lack of soap, hot water and bed linen. In one maternity hospital in Warsaw two women have to share a bed.

It is reported that in order to use the buildings for other purposes, the Germans ordered the inmates of mental hospitals and of hospitals for cripples and chronic invalids to be put to death. At the Chelmno Mental Hospital, 40 perfectly normal children were killed along with the 400 patients ; they were war orphans who had found a temporary refuge in the hospital.

II.   EFFECTS OF WAR CONDITIONS ON CHILDREN

Health, Nutrition and Growth

We have no detailed information bearing specially on these points, but the conditions described in the preceding chapter speak for themselves. They cannot but have the gravest effects upon the physical and mental development of the children as well as upon their emotional life.

Diseases

A recent report speaks of an increase in the number of cases of meningitis ; these appear to occur mainly among children who have been forced to witness public executions or the tortures inflicted on their parents.

An epidemic of typhus started in the ghetto of Warsaw in the summer of 1941 and spread to many other places. To combat the disease the Occupying Authorities appointed a special commissioner and district commissioners, who were given the help of 44 assistant doctors, 65 anti-epidemic and 65 disinfection units. The fight against typhus is, however, scarcely effective, since it does not attack the real causes of the trouble : overcrowding, the appalling sanitary conditions in the ghettos and the poor condition of the whole of the population which lacks fuel, linen and soap. There is not enough room in the hospitals nor means of transporting the sick there. It is impossible to take any preventive measures as no disinfecting apparatus is available. There is also a lack of anti-typhus vaccine, not enough even to immunise the whole of the staff of the sanitary units. On the black market one dose of anti-typhic injection costs as much as 1,000 zlotys.

The number of deaths due to diseases favoured, or caused by poor social conditions, has increased in the following proportion :

Christians : From 426 in August 1939 to   645 in August 1941
Jews :   From 141 ,,   ,,   ,,   ,, 1,643 ,,   ,,   ,,

Vital Statistics

The birth rate in Poland which, before the war, was one of the highest in Europe, is still high, but the death rate now far exceeds it.

Birth rate per 1,000 in Warsaw		Christians	Jews	Average
First half of 1939	..	77	101	84
„ „ 1941	..	64	38	55
Death rate per 1,000 in Warsaw				
First half of 1939	..	59	50	57
„ „ 1941	..	96	243	149

Education

In Poland elementary education was compulsory from seven to fourteen, and was considered a question of the first national importance. There were about 29,000 schools with five million pupils ; there were about 800 secondary schools, 28 universities or higher schools of university standing, and about 1,500 trades and agricultural schools of different types. About 100,000 children aged three to seven enjoyed physical and mental care in nearly 2,000 nursery schools. Younger children found shelter during day-time in day nurseries attached to each factory employing over one hundred women.

The situation differs in the General Government and in the areas incorporated in the Reich. In the incorporated area, Polish schools of all degrees and types have been closed. Polish children can receive some instruction in special German schools where the only subjects taught are the German language, arithmetic and gymnastics. Attendance at German schools has now been made compulsory for all Polish children born in 1933 or subsequently. The classrooms are badly overcrowded ; is is said that in Poznan, for instance, instruction is given in one classroom to as many as two hundred children. Polish teachers have been dismissed, if not shot, arrested, or expelled to the General Government. New German teachers are accepted without experience or training, if they conform to the standard set by Rust, the German Minister of Education. He is reported by the *Breslauer Neueste Nachrichten* of June 12, 1941, to have said, speaking at Katowice :

> ' The German elementary school teacher is far more like a political director than a professional teacher. He should work and lead among the people

and should behave more like a soldier than a man
from intellectual spheres'.

Private teaching, even lessons in the children's own
homes are forbidden and infractions of the rule are
punishable by death.

It is forbidden to sell Polish text-books, or for one
person to hand on any such book to another. Book-
sellers' stocks and most public and private libraries have
either been destroyed or carried off to Germany.

In western Poland, apprenticeship to artisans or in
factories is denied to Polish boys and girls who have
finished their elementary education. Every effort to
change the situation has been fruitless. ' No education
is needed to sweep the streets, or to dig potatoes, and other
occupations will be forbidden to the Poles ' was the
official answer of the German authorities at Torun in
November 1939.

In the General Government the number of Polish
elementary schools and of trade schools is altogether
insufficient. The latter exist almost exclusively in the
Warsaw and Cracow districts and provide only for about
60 per cent. of the number of pupils before the war, but
there they are taught merely the manual skill required
for the execution of work planned by others. The number
of elementary schools which are open varies considerably
according to the decisions of the Occupying Authorities.
It is understood that the number of children attending
elementary schools is not much more than half of what
it was before the war. In Warsaw, for instance, there
were 380 schools with 141,000 pupils in 1938, whereas
at the beginning of 1941 there were only 175 schools
with about 82,000 pupils. Further, lack of fuel and the
bad condition of buildings partly destroyed and summarily
repaired—if at all—are a great handicap to adequate
schooling. In these schools, all teaching of history,
geography and religion is forbidden; so also is the use of
Polish text-books for Polish language and literature, but
the study of German has been introduced. It is also
forbidden to publish new text-books, with the result
that there is a shortage of books even for the subjects

permitted. In the villages it is said that frequently children have to learn to read from their prayer-books.

In both the Incorporated Area and the General Government, all universities and secondary and the higher type of trade and technical schools have been closed, while public and private libraries, art collections, scientific laboratories, etc., have either been destroyed or carried away.

Religious instruction of the children * is made difficult in the Incorporated Area if not impossible by the fact that a large proportion of the priests has been arrested, and that those who remain are much restricted in their activity ; most churches have been closed.

In the diocese of Katowice, the German authorities refuse to allow Polish children to be prepared for Confession and First Communion in their own language. As only very few of the children have even the slightest knowledge of German, they are unable to receive the instruction necessary to prepare them for the Sacraments. In the diocese of Lodz, the teaching of religion in schools is forbidden.

Family Life and Dependency

Under the heading ' Movements of Population ', the arrest and deportation of many thousands of people, often without pretext, has been referred to. For the most trivial offence—for the breaking of a traffic regulation, for instance—or even without any apparent reason, anybody, man, woman, or child, may be arrested and subjected to a fate which means either slow or immediate death. According to German sources, over 70,000 people had been killed in that way up to January 1941. According to a statement of the Polish Minister of Home Affairs in London, on July 7, 1942, the number of Poles and Jews thus killed now reaches 400,000. Others, including children, are sent to concentration camps where, as is well known, the mortality is extremely high.

The atmosphere of perpetual suspense, of constant anxiety about one's nearest and dearest, caused by these frequent arrests and summary executions is one of the

---

* 93 per cent. of the Poles are Roman Catholics.

most painful experiences of the Polish family to-day.
If a father goes out to work, or a mother to do her
shopping, the family never knows if the parent will come
back or not, nor can those who go out ever tell if they will
find the family at home on their return.

Not only have many young people forcibly been sent
to Germany for work, but much younger children, even
babies of two and three years old, have been sent.
Instances are cited from Lodz, Ozorkow, Kalisz, Sieradz,
Bielsko in Silesia, and other towns and villages. The
number of such children is said to amount to thousands,
and it is believed that the intention is to Germanise them
completely. Many orphans, illegitimate children, or
foundlings have also been sent from the western
Provinces ; those of Jewish race have been sent to the
ghetto. This indiscrimate deportation of children
occurred mainly in 1939–40 ; from 1941, it affected
principally children over twelve.

Men, women and children are sent separately to work
in Germany, and the family is thus completely broken up.
No exceptions are made and there is no discrimination.
Cases are known of pregnant women and of mothers of
several children thus deported. Sometimes both parents
are taken and the children left to themselves. There
are, of course, no figures for the number of children thus
left alone. It is believed that these children as well as
orphans are cared for in the General Government in
orphanages, or through the existing system of foster
homes, or through the informal self-help organisations
that have sprung up everywhere.

Many children and young people have been killed
individually, or in groups, either as hostages or for some
offence such as wearing a Scout uniform. One finds a
description of many such painful incidents in the book
' The German New Order in Poland ', to which the reader
is again referred.

In the spring of 1940, there were many reports of
women and girls being rounded up in the streets, or
abducted from their homes or the shops, and either abused
sexually by men of the Army of Occupation or sent to
Germany.

Polish circles in Great Britain received, in June 1942, a description of the Helenowo Camp, near Lodz, for racial improvement, where young Polish boys and girls, aged 15 to 18, of good physique and perfect health are made to live in couples with German girls and boys of the same age.

'By September every hut in the camp was inhabited by a young pair : a German boy and a Polish girl or a Polish boy and a German girl.

'The camp day begins at 6 a.m. and finishes at 10 p.m. when lights must be put out in the little huts. There is no forced labour and the life is that of a well-run holiday camp. The boys and girls get meat every day, milk and fresh fruit as well as large quantities of white bread and fresh vegetables.

'But in spite of the seemingly complete freedom and of the good conditions in the camp, there is one duty which is absolutely compulsory—a duty from which none can escape. The couples living in the huts must have regular sexual intercourse, and this is strictly controlled by the camp doctor. Boys and girls failing to carry out their " duty " in this respect are severely punished.

'When Polish girls were forced to have relations with German boys there were attempts at suicide. In order to prevent them the spiritual leaders of the camp organised a series of special talks advocating sexual intercourse among the young people of the camp and showing the importance of racial purity in the German and Polish nations.

'The camp at Helenowo has recently been enlarged and there are now over 500 boys and girls, the majority of whom are Polish. The inmates are constantly being changed ; the girls who become pregnant are sent to Germany where they are to remain for good. The fate of the Polish girls after the birth of their child can easily be imagined. At the best they are either sent to work on the land or in an armament factory, while at the worst they will go to swell the ranks of the " women for the Army ".'

In a Decree of October 10, 1941, it is laid down that no Polish man under 28 and no woman under 25 may marry. This Decree, which applies to the three Incorporated Provinces, is supplemented by an order to the effect that any illegitimate child born to a woman under 25 shall be immediately placed in a State institution. The mother herself is liable to imprisonment.

The *Hamburger Fremdenblatt* of April 26, 1942, states that after this measure had been taken, the number of Polish marriages in the city of Lodz diminished in January and February 1942 by 82 per cent. as compared with the same period of 1941.

Juvenile Employment

According to Polish law, children could be employed only under the three following conditions : (1) agreement of the parents, (2) completion of the compulsory schooling, (3) fitness for the work chosen, ensured by careful medical examination. Certain industrial and other employments were absolutely forbidden to young people between 15 and 18 years on account of possible dangers to their moral and physical health. The work of juveniles was placed under certain safeguards and subjected to regular inspection. Overtime was not permitted. Young people were inspected medically at regular intervals to make sure that their health was not affected and, if necessary, their employment was changed, or they were sent for recuperation to a convalescent home.

All young workers and apprentices were entitled to 14 days' holiday after one year's work. It was compulsory for them to attend trade finishing-schools. For this purpose, they were to be given by their employer six hours per week with pay.* They were also covered by a complete system of social insurance.

The Occupying Authorities have suspended legislation concerning juvenile employment, especially for young people conscripted for labour who are now treated like adults. This applies in particular to hours of work. These have now been fixed at 60 per week, but in practice

---

* ' Workers' Protective Legislation in Poland,' with a Preface by Jan Stanczyk, Polish Minister of Labour, Liberty Publications, London, 1941.

it is often 72 or more. Wages have been maintained at pre war level in spite of the enormous increase in the cost of living, and social insurance benefits are greatly curtailed for workers of all ages. The granting of holidays with pay is now at the discretion of the management, which is either in German hands or under German control, the general rule being one week after three years' work.

Soon after the occupation Poles were urged to enrol for work in Germany, but although its voluntary character was stressed, mass arrests followed by deportation were carried out. However, compulsory labour was officially introduced only on 24th April 1942, by an order which makes it an offence not to register with the local Labour Exchange.

In the Incorporated Provinces also, juvenile Polish workers are treated as adults from 14 upwards.

A Decree of October 1941 prescribed that ration cards would only be delivered to people registered at the Labour Exchange. This measure is applicable to children from 12 years of age, for women up to 55, and for men up to 60. Many young people have either been deported to Germany or assigned to work in the local factories. At Ciechocinek, children were employed in the construction of a new cemetery.

If children and young people are sent to work in Germany, they are generally housed in huts in poor condition, they receive very little food and are made to work long hours, as much as 13 to 15 per day. They are subjected to various brutalities and humiliations, such as wearing a special mark, a letter P, in yellow embroidered on a violet ground, worn on the chest. Any friendly or even humane attitude towards them on the part of the local German population is strictly forbidden. They are made to do heavy work for a very low wage out of which, in addition to other taxes and charges, a special deduction of 15 per cent. is made—a deduction affecting only Poles. Another 2 per cent. is deducted for the Arbeitsfront, although no Pole may share in the benefits. They have no right to any social insurance in case of accident and sickness, nor to any form of social assistance to make up for

the lack of insurance benefits. All Polish welfare organisations which existed in Germany before the war were
abolished, while German welfare institutions are forbidden
to extend any help whatsoever to a Pole. As only a very
high temperature is considered as justifying an illness,
many cases of incipient tuberculosis are not recognised in
time and the unfortunate people are sent home when
it is too late for treatment.

At the end of August 1941, the Germans ordered boys
between the ages of 13 and 16 to present themselves at
the offices which arrange transportation to German labour
camps. They were checked by means of former Polish
school registers and sent directly to distribution centres
without being allowed to return home for warmer clothing ;
they were packed into goods vans—60 to each van—and
despatched to northern Germany, and to the Hanover and
Hamburg districts.

Compulsory labour is also organised in the General
Government under the term Baudienst ; the slightest
insubordination is severely punished ; attempts at escape
meet with the death penalty.

Recreation

There were many clubs for the children in pre-war
Poland, rest and reading centres, folkhouses, playgrounds,
summer and holiday camps. Their number grew steadily
from year to year. Thus in 1937, 450,000 children were
taken care of in whole-time or part-time summer camps
organised by welfare organisations, whilst an equal
number benefited from schemes organised by the schools
themselves.

Day nurseries were also organised for children under
seven in the villages during the period of most pressing
field work. In 1938 there were 2,109 such nurseries
with 25,707 children.

Now, not only is all this work stopped, but the best
playgrounds and most beautiful parks are reserved for
the Germans and no Polish child is allowed to enter.

The children suffer from the general starvation of
intellectual and artistic life. In the Incorporated Provinces, all cultural life for the Poles has been suspended.
All literary and artistic societies and choirs have been

dissolved Public and private libraries have been
plundered. All newspapers or periodicals in Polish
are forbidden, as well as the printing of books.

In the General Government the Germans themselves
print some newspapers in Polish, and by the Decree of
November 5, 1940, prohibit indefinitely publication of
any books, pamphlets, newspapers, periodicals, journals,
calendars and music, except such as are issued by the
General Government authorities. The sale of Polish
books is restricted and every manifestation of the better
kinds of literary or artistic activity is to be discouraged.

III. AMELIORATIVE MEASURES
*Survival and Efficiency of Pre-War Welfare and Health
    Services*

During the twenty years of independence, and starting
from conditions arising out of the appalling devastations
and epidemics consequent on the first World War, Poland
had built up its social and health services on very progressive lines. Unfortunately much of this work has now
either been destroyed or is in one way or another prevented from fulfilling its rôle as fully as circumstances
demand.

The social insurance system, which was considered a
model in Europe, has been seriously affected. It used to
help the worker and his dependants in case of (a) accident
and occupational diseases, (b) disease (including child
birth), (c) invalidity and old age, (d) unemployment.

The benefits given were either in kind, such as milk,
medicines, etc., or in the form of a lump sum of money
or of periodic payments. For instance, as regards health
insurance, the benefits included medical assistance,
medical supplies, and the cost of hospital or other treatment for the insured person and any member of his
family. Women, during pregnancy and child-birth,
received medical and hospital treatment, as well as a sub-
sistence allowance during the eight weeks following
confinement. After that, the mother received a quart
of milk free daily. The confinement allowance was
75 per cent. of the normal income of the insured person
as compared with 60 per cent. in the case of illness.

UNIVERSITY
COLLEGE
LIBRARY
NOTTINGHAM

Another boon for mothers and babies were the rest homes in the country open all the year round, to which they could go for recuperation.

Juvenile workers received the same benefits as adults in the case of accidents or occupational diseases. If the insured person died, his widow, children or dependent parents received the pension that would have been due to him.

Now unemployment insurance has been abolished, whilst in the other three groups benefits are restricted to the worker himself and his dependants are helped no longer,

In 1940 the average amount of sickness and maternity benefits paid out to 100 people was 40 per cent. less than before the war; the amount spent on medicines, surgical appliances, and so on, 42 per cent. less; and the number of medical consultations given 28 per cent. less. These numbers are all the more significant as, owing to the ravages of war, the need for medical assistance was certainly greater in 1940 than before the war.

Relief of the destitute was the joint responsibility of the State, the local authorities and the voluntary associations.

Because of the conditions described above, expulsions, executions, deportations, etc., many families have lost their breadwinner. On the other hand, many breadwinners have lost their proper jobs, especially in the professional classes and officials. About two million people are deprived of any means of existence. These circumstances, and the very low and entirely inadequate wages of those who work, are the causes for which a large proportion of the population is in need of social assistance. But, as a result of the occupation, the State contributions, in the form of considerable grants to all manner of social organisations, have entirely ceased, while the local authorities, though they are permitted to organise and carry on social relief in the General Government, can do so only inadequately in view of the prevailing conditions. One of the few Polish official bodies still allowed to function in the General Government by the Germans is that of the Health and Social Welfare Centres. These supplied treatment in clinics, and also provided nurses to carry on treatment in patients' homes, and in some cases administered poor relief.

In so far as the buildings have not been destroyed or requisitioned for other purposes, the centres are still working, at least in the larger towns. Their work is, however, hampered by the lack of medicines, dressings, surgical appliances, etc., and the general conditions prevailing, so that, in spite of increased distress, they cared for 84,634 persons in 1941, compared with 84,086 in 1936–37.

In addition, through the Municipal Assistance Boards (Rada Opieckuncza Miejska = R.O.M.) 216,825 people received (July 1941) occasional help mainly in the form of meals in soup kitchens. The Boards are not, however, in a position to give the meals free of charge, the contribution of an average family being about 20 zlotys per month, whilst at the same time the food value of the meal is much diminished.

In the Incorporated Provinces, even the local health services have ceased functioning, as all the administration was taken over by the Germans, who refuse any assistance to Poles. If Poles have no right to social assistance in the incorporated areas, however, the Volksdeutsche, *i.e.* the local inhabitants who declare themselves as being Germans, benefit from various social measures, including, for instance, admission of their children to kindergartens on equal terms with German children, and better food rations. Thus a certain amount of pressure is put on groups of Poles to make them declare themselves as Germans.

In the General Government, voluntary associations carried on for a certain time with their limited means until the Occupying Authorities decided that all private welfare efforts had to be centralised in a central welfare board. This body is, however, not in a position to provide the various institutions with the means (money and goods) necessary for the carrying out of their aims.

The action of the few voluntary associations which survive is hampered by lack of means, and also by the fact that many social leaders—men and women—have been interned in concentration camps, and that the funds of many of them have been confiscated.

In the Incorporated Area all voluntary social organisations have been suppressed. The many Catholic institutions have also been closed, and their staffs expelled to the General Government, imprisoned, or executed.

The fate of the abnormal and crippled children, like that of the aged and of chronic invalids, is terrible. The institutions in which they were cared for have been closed, sometimes after the inmates had been killed (see the case of the Chelmo Mental Hospital, page 91). In some places, in February 1940, those who lived with their families had to be registered and were then collected, driven away, and never heard of any more.

The solidarity of the Poles is one of the most remarkable factors in the situation. Even the poorest of peasants will take into their homes the people expelled from the Incorporated Areas. Unofficial self-help committees are springing up among small groups, such as the inhabitants of one street or of a block of houses, or between the employees of a factory or of a business firm. These self-help activities are, however, discouraged by the German authorities.

War Relief

Certain organisations for social assistance which have been founded before the invasion, have been allowed to continue. Their means are, however, hopelessly inadequate to meet the needs and they are allowed to give relief only in kind, *i.e.* mainly through meals in public kitchens. There are 124 such kitchens giving 110,000 meals daily at Warsaw alone, but the cost of living is rising at such a speed that the caloric value of the meals is correspondingly declining and is as low as 160 to 180 calories. (A normal adult requires 2,400 calories a day.) Although there is great need of clothing, these organisations are not able to give much warm clothing. The total number helped by is not known, but according to reports on their activity in April and May 1942, it included more than a million people expelled from their homes. It is estimated, however, that the number of people needing assistance is two million.

During the winter of 1939-40, a certain amount of relief was brought to the population of the General Government by American Friends and other American bodies. The International Red Cross was able to forward during the winter of 1941-42, with funds provided by the Papal Nuncio in Bern, about 30 tons of peas and millet, and a certain amount of milk foods and Ovaltine. It also sent medicines and anti-typhus vaccine to various benevolent institutions. In the early summer of 1942 it arranged for the transport from Lisbon of 36 tons of medicines sent by the Commission for Polish Relief.

IV. THE CONDITION OF THE JEWS

General Conditions

There were, in the whole of Poland before the war, 3,115,000 Jews, of whom 1,214,000 (or 39 per cent.) were in the territory occupied by the U.S.S.R. in 1939.

Jews were, of course, among the first to be expelled from the incorporated areas, and nearly all of them have been forced into the General Government, mainly into the Lublin district, where a Jewish reservation was to be created.   Moreover, similar steps were also taken in parts of the General Government itself, for instance in Cracow, from which all Jews were ordered to leave before August 18, 1940, under threat of becoming liable to compulsory labour service.

Later, however, the idea of concentrating the whole Jewish population of Poland in the Lublin district was abandoned and ghettos were arranged in any city of the General Government which had a fairly large Jewish population. To these ghettos Jews from other districts have to move. The conditions of overcrowding cannot be exaggerated ; for instance, in Warsaw, in blocks of flats which originally housed 90 people, nearly 400 now have to live, which works out at an average of 13 persons per room, instead of the pre-war 2·1. The ghettos are completely closed and only a limited amount of food is allowed in—this in exchange for manufactured goods. A Council of Elders handles all questions of internal administration under the supervision of the German authorities*.

Of the 540,000 inhabitants of the Warsaw ghetto about three-quarters are unable to do any kind of work because of their age or their health, thus leaving about 135,000 who have to work in some way to provide for the others. There were in the area a few factories, workshops and retail shops ; but the difficulty of getting tools, raw materials and goods, and the control of the Transferstelle (the official agency for economic exchanges with the outer world) make it almost impossible for the individual to carry on his business. A co-operative system, both for production and for distribution, has therefore been much encouraged by the Council of Elders to meet this difficulty and has now been made more or less compulsory by the German authorities. Salaries are, however, very low. In some of the co-operative undertakings which are working for the Germans, the situation of the Jewish workers is slightly better since they receive additional food rations.

The theoretical amount of rations is not known ; they are, however, lower than those of the Poles, whilst the prices are almost double.

Among the professional Jews, only doctors employed in hospitals or clinics, and nurses and engineers are permitted to continue their work. As from March 1940, Jews may be attended by Jewish doctors only. According to information which reached London in June 1942, medical assistance in the ghettos is now forbidden to children under five, and to adults over 45.

According to the *Hamburger Fremdenblatt* of October 29, 1940, of the cases of typhoid and spotted fever, 98 per cent. occurred in the ghetto of Warsaw. The Delegation of the American Joint Distribution Committee reported that all but 8 per cent. of the typhoid cases in Warsaw were among the Jewish population. Concurrently with other measures to combat typhus, the German authorities decreed that any Jews leaving the ghetto without per-

---

* For fuller details on the conditions of life in the ghettos, the reader is referred to ' The Ghetto of Warsaw ', by Dr. Manfred Sachs, London, 1942.

mission would be killed on the spot. Soon afterwards thirty vagrant children who had escaped from the Warsaw ghetto were publicly drowned in a pool at the Glymianski brickworks.

In spite of the fact that deaths are much more numerous than births, the population in the ghetto does not diminish, as there is a continual influx of Jews expelled from those provincial districts in which the Germans do not propose to set up separate Jewish quarters.

The Children

In August and September 1941, the Jewish health organisation (TOZ) carried out in the Warsaw ghetto an examination of some 23,000 children, under the supervision of 11 doctors and 17 nurses. 12,164 children were examined in August and 11,530 in September. The results were as follows :

	August per cent.	September per cent.
Diet :		
Satisfactory	13	14
Average	35	26
Poor	52	60
Cleanliness :		
Clean	58	50
Dirty	23	30
Infested with lice	19	20

Among the children examined, 4,130 (34 per cent.) in August, and 2,803 (24 per cent.) in September were in need of medical treatment. In September there were 178 children suffering from boils caused by malnutrition. This examination covered only part of the 31,000 children registered with TOZ, and does not include those who were not able to be treated because of lack of medicine, shortage of room in the hostels, and so on.

On August 31, 1940, Governor-General Frank issued a Decree concerning Jewish schools in the General Government. This Decree made it obligatory for the Council of Elders to provide schools. They had to establish the necessary number of elementary schools and were empowered to establish technical schools. They must also provide for the training of teachers.

The Jewish schools are to be regarded as private schools but, although the authorities do not contribute to their upkeep, the German Department of Education is entitled to supervise them.   Jews are allowed to go to their own schools only.   Those in the Warsaw ghetto were re-opened in April 1941, but they are in very poor condition.   Only about 5,000 children were attending them in the summer of 1941.

The only place where the Jewish children of Warsaw can see grass and trees is the cemetery.

YUGOSLAVIA *

I. GENERAL CONDITIONS

Conditions in Yugoslavia are believed to be distressing in every respect.   How far these conditions affect the lives of the children, even responsible circles of the Yugoslav Government have but scanty means of knowing.

For this there are many reasons : the country is almost completely cut off from the outer world—very few people managing to escape and little information seeping through ; it is divided into many parts under different régimes, so that such information as gets through is for the most part only of local value ; finally, in large areas guerrilla fighting still continues.

Northern Slovenia has been annexed by Germany and the remainder attached to Croatia which, in theory, is independent, but part of that country has been annexed by Italy, the rest being under the joint control of Italy and Germany.   Montenegro is occupied by Italy ; a strip of country north of Belgrade has been annexed by Hungary ; Serbian Macedonia is partly annexed, partly occupied by the Bulgarians, whilst Serbia itself (with four million inhabitants) with the Banat (700,000 inhabitants) has its own Government but is occupied by German troops.   Much fighting continues in the mountains of Montenegro, Bosnia, Herzegovina and Novi-Bazar, sometimes extending to within a few miles of the capital.

* Part of the information about Yugoslavia has kindly been supplied by Mr. B. Pepic, of the Information Department of the Royal Yugoslav Government.

Population

According to the 1931 census, the Yugoslav population numbered 13,974,000. Of these 34·6 per cent., *i.e.* 4,825,000, were under 15.

Economic Conditions

War and the Occupation, and the breaking-up of the country into seven different economic and political territories, make the feeding of the population a matter of extreme difficulty.

According to reports received by the Yugoslav Government, and to statements made by the Occupying Authorities themselves, 30 per cent. of the agricultural area is not now cultivated at all. The remaining 70 per cent. is insufficiently cultivated because of the deportation of the peasants, the shortage of seeds and the lack of fertilisers and, above all, the economic sabotage by the peasants, who will sow no more than they need for themselves. It is a fair estimate that the total agricultural production of the country is not more than 50 per cent. of the pre-war output.

The reduction, both in the quantities of foodstuffs available to consumers and in the amounts consumed, is due to a number of facts :

(a) All stocks previously laid in are exhausted ;

(b) Guerrilla warfare extends over a great part of the country ;

(c) Great quantities of the crops were exported to Germany by the occupying authorities from the Vojvodina, Srijem, and East Slovenia—regions which formerly supplemented the insufficient production of other areas in the country ;

(d) The occupying forces, some 450,000, must be fed ;

(e) For political and economic reasons peasants will neither bring their produce to market nor, in spite of the severest penalties, allow their produce to be requisitioned ;

(f) Transport is seriously hampered by guerrilla warfare.

Movements of Population

The greatest movements of population seem to have taken place in Slovenia. The number of Slovenes deported from their homes to various countries in Europe or to other parts of Yugoslavia amounts, according to Yugoslav sources, to about 160,000, of whom some 20,000 were sent to Croatia and settled on the properties of Serbs who were killed or expelled. Some 60,000 were sent to Serbia and the rest to Poland and Germany.

The Serbs driven out of Croatia, and those expelled from the territory annexed by Hungary, amount to many tens of thousands. They had to leave their homes at a few hours' notice ; children were separated from their parents who, in many cases, have not yet been able to trace them.

From Italian-annexed Slovenia, and mainly from the Ljubljana district, people of German nationality or citizenship were ordered to be transported to Germany in November 1941. We have no information as to the conditions under which these movements of population took place.

In every part of the country controlled by Germany workers are invited to volunteer for work in the Reich. This is the case in Serbia as well as in Croatia. From the latter, 130,000 workmen are reported to have gone up to June 1942.

In Slovenia, men and boys are forcibly recruited, and girls aged 15 to 25 are enrolled as ' F.M.M.' (Freies Militär Mädchen).

Food

Rationing is known to have been introduced throughout the greater part of the country—200 grammes of cereals per head being allowed, *i.e.* one-fifth of the normal consumption, though even that small quantity cannot be regularly supplied to the population. According to repeated admissions by representatives of the occupying Governments, famine exists in the country. From Dalmatia and Montenegro deaths from hunger are reported in increasing numbers.

The situation is also clearly seen from the enormously steep increase in prices fixed by the authorities in Serbia, as follows:

	August 1939	April 1941	December 1941
	(Dinars per 100 kilogrammes)		
Wheat	143	300	450
Maize	117	250	350
Meat	900	1,100	1,500
Lard	1,375	3,200	6,400
Fat swine	950	1,300	3,400

Black market prices are from five to ten times greater.

Croatia also is reported to be suffering from food shortage and high prices. It is said that wheat was 450 kunas* per 100 kilogrammes in August 1941, an increase of 200 per cent. over the previous year.

Lard and other fats were generally used for cooking in pre-war Yugoslavia ; a shortage of butter, which is not an essential article of food (except in a few towns) does not necessarily imply a shortage of fats. Lard, however, is very scarce, and although the people are allowed 400 grammes a month in Serbia, it is almost impossible to buy it because the occupying authorities have depleted the country of all its stocks of pigs.

The bread contains a good deal of maize. Fuel shortage made the bread situation more acute in Belgrade and other Serbian towns last winter, since sometimes bakers could not produce any bread for a full fortnight owing to lack of fuel. Not only can the nominal rations not always be had, but very little other food such as macaroni, rice, milk, and salt, is obtainable, except on the black market at exorbitant prices. According to *Novo Vreme* of April 2, 1942, the police have imposed the maximum of one cooked meal a day for each person in Belgrade ; meat meals are allowed only on Saturdays and Sundays.

For tables of weekly rations see Appendix.

Clothing

In Serbia, adults can buy up to the value of 1,200 dinars a month, and children up to 14 years of age 600 dinars.

In Croatia no person having more than two suits, or overcoats, or dresses, may buy new ones. Customers must give a detailed written statement of what they have.

* 1 Kuna=1 dinar=approximately 6d. in 1939.

Soap

The monthly ration is nominally 50 grammes (1¾ oz.), but in fact during the year April 1941 to March 1942, soap was distributed only twice.

Fuel

The serious coal shortage in Belgrade last winter has already been referred to. Electricity was cut off between 7.30 a.m. and 6 p.m., except in the case of hospitals, waterworks, etc. ; trains could not run and schools were closed. (Budapest message quoted in *Arbetaren*, Stockholm, November 17, 1941.)

II. EFFECTS OF WAR CONDITIONS ON CHILDREN

Health

Very little precise information about health conditions is available, but it is significant that (according to reliable information) there are children in the town of Sabac, in Serbia, who have lost their eyesight from lack of suitable food.

Education

It has already been stated that schools were closed in Belgrade last winter owing to the shortage of fuel, but it seems that throughout the whole of Serbia children have no regular education, owing to the general unrest. Many teachers have been arrested and even children have had to pay with their lives for being found with illegal papers. On October 21, 1941, the pupils of the three upper forms of the Kragujevac Secondary School, 80 miles south of Belgrade, about a hundred in number, with their teachers and the headmaster, were marched from their class-rooms to make up the required number of hostages to be shot as reprisals. Some of them tried instinctively, we are told, to protect themselves from the bullets with their satchels or their text-books. In most schools all attempts at teaching were given up after that tragedy.

In Croatia, schooling seems less disturbed, although buildings are frequently requisitioned. Great importance is given to German schools and to the teaching of German. According to a Decree of June 21, 1941, there is to be a

German elementary school wherever there are more than 20 German children within a radius of eight kilometres. Where there are only between 10 to 20 children within the same radius, an auxiliary school has to be set up, and when there are less than 10 children an educational unit (Schulstutzpunkt). These schools will, of course, use the German language as the medium of instruction, and will impress upon pupils the importance of the National-Socialist Weltanschauung. Croat subjects, however, such as history, civics, and the Croat language, will be taught in Croat by Croat teachers.

In Slovenia little is known about the educational position. All Yugoslav schools have been closed, as they were in the territories annexed to Hungary and Bulgaria. The Church, which played a great part in the lives of the Roman Catholic Slovenes, is seriously persecuted ; only seven out of 474 priests in the diocese of Maribor, for instance, being left at liberty. All religious ceremonies, including marriage and baptism, are forbidden.

Dependent Children
Although there are no figures available, it seems certain that guerrilla fighting and the ensuing reprisals have robbed many children of their parents and others of their homes. Villages and towns have been destroyed either wholly or in part, and their population decimated or killed in even higher proportions, for instance, 5,000 persons in Kraljevo, 2,300 in Kragujevac, etc. According to the *Stockholms Tidningen* of March 1, 1942, one hundred Serbians are liable to be taken as hostages and shot for each German killed. There is said to be a large number of vagrant and neglected children, those who had their homes in districts from which the population were driven out, or where guerrilla war and reprisals are still raging.

Youth Organisations
In order that schoolboys may ' employ their youthful energy usefully', the Ministry of Education has formed a special middle school labour-camp in Serbia. Members are not exempt from subsequent duty in the National Labour Service. (*Novo Vreme*, February 14, 1942.)

H

An Ustasa (Croat terrorist) youth organisation has been formed in Croatia, consisting of three groups ; for boys of 7 to 11, of 11 to 15, and of 15 to 21 years respectively.

III. AMELIORATIVE MEASURES

Much of the activity of the pre-war health and social services is believed to have been seriously disturbed, either deliberately, or from force of circumstances.

The National Red Cross is still carrying on under the title of the Serbian Red Cross (formerly the Yugoslav Red Cross). Early in 1942 it distributed tinned milk and other foods, as well as some medicines sent from Switzerland by the International Red Cross, and so far as is known this is the only relief to have reached Serbia.

A group of 500 Serbian children invited to spend three months in Switzerland to recuperate arrived in that country at the end of May 1942. They were the first batch from Yugoslavia to receive this help.

FINLAND*

I. GENERAL CONDITIONS

Population

This country, larger in area than Great Britain, has a total population less than that of Switzerland ; *i.e.* 3,864,000, of whom 985,200 or about 25·5 per cent. are under 15 years of age.

Economic Situation

Agriculture.—In spite of the small population, Finland is unable, by reason of her soil and climate, to be self-supporting agriculturally. In the north, vast regions are unfit for cultivation, while further south, thousands of lakes, marshy ground and immense forests—though the latter are a source of wealth—diminish the extent of arable land. Moreover the severity of the climate limits

---

* Most of the information is taken from a report that Dr. R. Hercod, Director of the International Bureau against Alcoholism, Lausanne (Switzerland), drew up after a visit to Finland in January-February 1942, during which, at the request of the Save the Children International Union, he inquired into the conditions of life for children.

the yield of crops, so that Finland, except as regards dairy produce, cannot live without imported food. Great efforts have been made to increase agricultural production and also to develop industry, of which the products could be exchanged against foodstuffs. As a result, although the standard of life has always been extremely simple, it was, before the war, comfortable enough. In the south, at least, a high cultural level had been reached throughout the population.

There is grave concern about this year's harvest as very little seed was available this spring, especially for the recovered part of Karelia. For this district Germany has promised 2,000 tons of seed potatoes.

In 1940 the number of hens had decreased from about 2,800,000 (in 1939) to 1,200,000 and it is assumed that now (1942) they are not more than 12 to 20 per cent. of the pre-war number. (In 1937 about half the total egg production was available for export.) The reason for this decrease is that people are now obliged to eat what was formerly used as hen food.

The cost of living rose by nearly 79 per cent., between August 1939, and December 1941, according to an article in *Dagens Nyheter*, published in Stockholm on April 2, 1942. Imported goods have risen by 110 per cent. ; home-produced goods by 66 per cent. Wages have not been increased in the same proportion.

Movements of Population

The war with Russia in the winter of 1939–40 not only strained the country's resources but deprived it of Karelia, one of the richest provinces and also one of the most densely populated. About half a million refugees fled from this district during the Russian war, most of them without any property save what they could carry. The resettlement of so large a proportion of the population in a poor country presented a grave problem. The difficulties were further increased by the Russian invasion, the blockade and the disorganisation consequent on war. Before the country had time for recovery, it was again at war.

During the war of 1939–40, Finland had organised the voluntary evacuation of children from the towns to the country. The tradition of family care for orphans and other dependent children is so strong that it was possible to billet children in fairly good conditions. We have no information as to the actual numbers evacuated, nor do we know whether this first large-scale evacuation was repeated during the second war.

Food

During the winter of 1941–42 it was generally possible to obtain the amounts shown in the Appendix, but the standard war-time adult ration allows only for about 1,500 calories a day instead of the normal 2,500 to 2,800. In the very cold northern winter, much richer food is necessary to maintain health than in more temperate climates, and the Finns used to consume very large quantities of milk, butter and other dairy products. The deficiency of these foods affects them very adversely. They also miss the citrus fruits which used to be imported free of duty to compensate for the almost complete absence of native fruit, save for the wild berries that grow plentifully in the forests. Similarly, very few vegetables can be grown. Thus people have now to depend mostly on bread and potatoes, which do not provide a diet adequate either in quantity or variety. Of such fat as is still obtainable, larger quantities are allotted to children and to nursing mothers than to ordinary people. This is naturally the case with milk also.

No fishing is possible in winter, since the sea and the lakes are frozen. And even in the season of open-water, fishing is now restricted, as there is no string with which to mend the nets.

According to information published in Finnish and Swedish papers during March and April 1942, the food situation seems to have deteriorated greatly since Dr. Hercod's visit. Even potatoes, which were with bread (as he said) the staple food of the people, have disappeared from the market, at least in Helsinki and other large cities, and none were expected until the 1942 harvest. Only small quantities of carrots and turnips were available. It was also announced that meat would practically disappear during the summer months and already in March it had not been possible to get more than a pound of fish of meat per head at Helsinki as the ration for the whole month. It was expected that, with the thaw and the consequent resumption of water transport, the bread situation would be eased.

Viborg people were warned that they would get very little milk during the summer, as there are no refrigerator vans on the railway in which to bring it from the Lahti district, from whence it was obtained during the winter.

Newspapers make frequent complaints of hoarding and black-marketing. Potatoes were still to be had in April in the black market at 500–700 marks* a hectolitre (2¾ bushels) ; butter at 300 marks per kilogramme ; coffee at 1,200 to 2,000 marks per kilogramme. It is said, further, that some farmers do not deliver their milk to the dairies but keep it to make butter for sale in the black market.

During the winter some small consignments of Italian lemons and oranges and of Spanish oranges arrived at Finnish ports, but they had been so long on the journey and were so badly affected by the cold that part of them was unfit for consumption. See comparative table in the Appendix for weekly rations for May 1942.

Clothing

Woollen and cotton materials are equally rare, as also are shoes and the rubber boots which had become extremely popular during recent years.

Textiles are so scarce that the layettes provided by the State for mothers under a certain income level are made now almost entirely of paper, with a few cotton articles but no woollen. The Ministry of Social Welfare recommends them, but nurses and midwives find them unsatisfactory.

Soap

The soap ration is only 125 grammes (4½ oz.) for three months or 250 grammes (9 ozs.) of washing powder. The ration is double for children born after 1937. The dearth of soap is a special hardship for Finns who normally keep themselves, their clothes, and their homes extraordinarily clean. A steam bath with plenty of soap at least once a week was the rule even in the poorest rural home.

*1 Finnish mark=about 1d. in 1939

Fuel

No information is available.

Medical Supplies

There is a great dearth of medical supplies. The director of the main children's hospital of Helsinki showed Dr. Hercod many little patients doomed to die because the proper treatment could not be given. Tonics, vitamin preparations and semi-medicinal foods are completely lacking.

II. EFFECTS OF WAR CONDITIONS ON CHILDREN

Nutrition, Health and Growth

It is estimated that a large proportion of the children of Finland, at least in the towns, are seriously underfed. Professor Ylpöö, a children's doctor of world fame, told Dr. Hercod that this is true for probably 50 per cent. No statistics, however, are yet available, and it is believed that, as children were normally very well cared for in Finland and parents still do their utmost to obviate hardships, it will take some time for the consequences of the present conditions to become apparent.   However, the Chief Medical Officer of Health for Schools stated that undernourishment and fatigue are adversely affecting their studies (*Suomen Sosialidemokraatti*, March 25, 1942). Conditions are said to be much worse since the winter of 1941–42 ; children often faint in the class rooms and there are queues of them outside the food kitchens.

In the school Dr. Hercod visited at Viborg in January, he found the children looking rather pale, tired and listless, but, with a characteristic repugnance for exaggeration, his companions begged him not to generalise, since Viborg children had suffered special hardships, three-fourths of the town having been gutted.

It was extremely difficult, Dr. Hercod was told, to find sufficient variety of foodstuffs for the school canteen.

Conditions are said to be much worse in Eastern Karelia, because it has been the scene of fighting during the two wars.

Diseases and Mortality

So far there are no statistics showing a definite increase of disease, although specialists speak of an increase of tuberculosis in children (mostly tubercular meningitis).

It is further reported that infant mortality, especially neo-natal mortality, is increasing, but again we have no definite figures for guidance.

Education

No information is available.

Family Life

Most of the men being in the Army, women are called upon for a great variety of civilian jobs, with the result that children are left very much to look after themselves. The younger ones are deprived of the care they need and the older ones run wild far too early. Funds are lacking to supply the day nurseries and play-rooms that are urgently required.

Dependency

Finland has already to provide for about 20,000 war orphans. In accordance with the national custom, they are not assembled in orphanages but placed in foster-homes, under careful supervision and with the financial assistance of the State. In many cases the care of these children is combined with the resettlement of refugees from Karelia (see Section III).

III. AMELIORATIVE MEASURES

Survival and Efficiency of Pre-War Services

In matters of child welfare, Finland was a most progressive country. State and private organisations were equally concerned to give every child a good start in life. It seems, however, that the wars have absorbed so much of the national resources that the State can no longer adequately cope with the increased needs of children and young people, and that most of the voluntary associations are in similar plight, except the Mannerheim League— the national association for the care of mothers and children which is attached to the Red Cross.

Relief and Other War Measures

At the outbreak of war a national organisation, Suomen Huolto, was founded to centralise and co-ordinate all relief, both national and foreign. Great sympathy was shown to Finland during the first war by many countries which sent funds, goods of all descriptions, medical units, and so on. The other Scandinavian countries, and especially Sweden, were most generous. Sweden is now practically the only country still able to help on an appreciable scale.

The main Swedish relief committee, Samarbets-Committen för nordisk Hjälparbete, did not specialise in children's work, but Rädda Barnen, the Swedish Save the Children Fund, collected many hundred thousand kroner, and huge quantities of clothing and other goods. Most of the funds were used to settle Karelian refugee families with many children in special colonies which are described below, and to bring help to individual children. About 10,800 children had been so helped up to December 31, 1941, for a total value of 1,500,000 Swedish kroner.

The Swedish Committee for Aid to Finnish Children, whose representative in Finland is Dr. Nyberg, has made plans to feed at least 10,000 children in Helsinki and other towns. In April 1942, it had already collected two million marks (about £1,000) and hoped to reach five million. It was first intended to open 15 canteens only but desperate appeals were received from many places, and in June 1942, 6,000 children, and a few nursing and pregnant mothers, received free meals in 22 localities. The foodstuffs for these meals : sausages, cereals, black-puddings, sugar, and macaroni, are to come mainly from Denmark, but will be paid for by the Swedish Committee ; pea-flour for soup, and vegetable preparations rich in vitamins from Hungary.

Up to date, about 20,000 children have gone to Sweden to recuperate for a few months. They are mostly placed free of charge in families. The committee gives, however, a small grant to suitable families who cannot afford to take children free, and thus enables them to play their part in this very popular relief action. (Some children are still cared for by Denmark, and it was anticipated that more would be sent there in the summer months when travelling would be easier.) Since January 1942, Sweden has also been receiving sick children, mostly tubercular patients, for whom under present conditions there is neither room nor the requisite treatment in Finnish hospitals.

Responsible people, both Swedish and Finnish, would prefer that relief should be given direct to children in Finland itself, as that would be the surest way to ensure a fair distribution. The blockade makes it impossible at present.

It is proposed to evacuate all children under 15 from Helsinki for the summer. Those of an age to do so are expected to help on the farms. Girls over 15 will be thus employed, whilst boys over 15 who are not already working or do not volunteer for farm or forestry work will probably come under a compulsory labour scheme.

Most of the families which fled from Karelia during the winter and spring of 1940, have been resettled on the land through a scheme of internal colonisation. They have been given land, houses, tools, livestock and seeds, and with this help it was hoped that they would be self-supporting in the minimum of time.

An interesting and successful experiment was carried out by Dr. Nyberg, the general secretary of the Central Union for Children and Young People (member organisation of the Save the Children International Union) with funds received from the Union, and from Rädda Barnen; colonies were founded for evacuees and orphans, in which over 700 war orphans and a few war widows have found shelter and a normal home life. In these colonies, war orphans are boarded with suitable peasant families, who have additional bedding and other equipment lent them free by the committee. When these children still have a mother, she is included in the scheme. In that case, peasants are persuaded to lend rent free one of their farm out-buildings (one at least is generally equipped with a stove and chimney), and the committee provides the necessary household furniture and equipment. Karelian war widows who have five children or more are settled in these buildings and are given a few war orphans to take care of. Their own pensions (ten Finnish marks* a day) supplemented by those of the children (eight Finnish marks for each of the first two children, seven for the others) have enabled them to live decently if very simply. Most of them are now able, with the help of their older children, to be self-supporting.

The headquarters of the colony, established in a central village, comprises a simple lodging for the supervisor, a clinic, sick bay, clothing dépôt, etc., whilst in each village a health visitor supervises the families and watches over their moral and material well-being, the regularity of school attendance, friendly relations with the local population, and so on. When the second war broke out, about 250 more children were easily billeted in the colonies.

APPENDIX

RATIONING

In the occupied countries the bread ration is, as a rule, calculated by the day and other commodities by the month. The following tables show in every case the weekly averages which are expressed, in the first column in grammes and litres, the metric weights and measures actually employed and, in the second column for the convenience of English readers, in the equivalent pounds, ounces or pints.

If not otherwise specified the rations for children are the same as those for adults.

To appreciate these tables properly other points must be borne in mind. If commodities are not mentioned it generally means, with the exception of Denmark, not that they are plentiful but, on the contrary, that they are so scarce as not to be worth rationing. Amounts shown indicate therefore not a minimum but a maximum, rarely reached, supplies being generally not large enough to allow purchasers to get the amounts to which nominally they are entitled.

---

* 1 Finnish mark = about 1d. in 1939.

TABLES OF WEEKLY RATIONS

BELGIUM (May 1942)

	Normal Consumer		Children		Notes
	grammes	lb. oz.	grammes	oz.	
Bread ..	1,575	3 7			Flour, biscuits.
Cereal					diet foods, etc,
products	70	2½			on bread cou-
					pons
Potatoes ..	3,500	7 11			Sometimes less
					than one-fifth
					available in
					large cities
Pulses ..	60	2			
Sugar ..	230	8	0–1 : 350	12½	
Jam ..	105	4			
Artificial					
honey	70	2½			
Fats ..	92	3½			
Meat (includ-ing 20 per cent. bones)	175	6			
Chicory ..	30	1			
			litres	pints	
Whole milk .	none		0–3 : 5·25	9½	Nursing
			3–6 : 3·5	6	mothers :
			6–14 : 1·75	3	5·25 (9½ pints)
Skimmed milk	locally rationed				

CZECHOSLOVAKIA (PROTECTORATE) (after April 13, 1942)

	Normal Consumer		Children and Young People			Notes
	grammes	lb. oz.	age	gms.	lb. oz.	
Bread ..	2,000	4 8	0–6	1,000	2 4	
			6–14	1,700	3 13	
			14–20	2,600	5 13	
Cereals .	none		0–6	250	8	
Barley .	37·5	1½				
Potatoes	2,500	5 8				
Pulses..	62·5	2				
Sugar ..	250	8	0–6	267·5	9	
or			6–14	262	9	
Sugar }	75	3				
and jam }	350	12½				
Butter..	none		0–6	125	4½	
			6–14	100	3½	
			14–20	50	2	
Other			0–6	none		
fats	163	6	6–14	100	3½	
			14–20	150	6	
Meat ..	300	10½				
Eggs ..	one					
Chicory	100	3½				
	litres	pints		litres	pints	Fat content
Milk ..	1·75	3	0–6	: 3·5	6	reduced from
						3·6 to 2·5 per
						cent.

NOTE.—The following additional foodstuffs are distributed in the territories incorporated in the Reich :—

Dried fruit (up to 5 oz.) and cheese (1 oz.)

And for children under 6 only :—

Sweets (2 oz.), artificial honey (4 oz.), and oranges (1 lb.) or apples (2 lb.).

DENMARK (April 1920)

	Normal Consumer		Children under 6		Notes
	grammes	lb. oz.	grammes	lb. oz.	
Bread ..	2,200	5	1,100	2½	
Breakfast Oats or Barley Flour	250	9 9			
Potatoes ..	Unrationed				
Sugar ..	500	1 1½			
Fats	315	11			
Meat	Unrationed but		one meat less day		a week
Milk	Unrationed				
Tea .. ⎫ Coffee ⎬ Chocolate ⎭	Unobtainable				

FRANCE (April 1942)

	Normal Consumer		Children and Young People			Notes
	grammes	lb. oz.	age	grms.	lb. oz.	
Bread ..	1,925	4 4	0–3	1,700	1 9	
			3–6	1,400	3 2	
			6–13	1,925	4 4	
			13–20	2,450	5 7	
Flour ⎫ Cereals ⎪ Biscuits ⎬ Semolina ⎪ etc. ⎭	on specifi	ed brea	d coupons			
Potatoes..	Locally	ratione	d : 500 to 2,000		gramme	s
		o	r 1 lb. to 4½ lb.			
Rice ..	no	ne	0–3	70	2½	Winter only
			3–6	45	1½	
Macaroni or tapioca	60	2				Winter only
Sugar ..	125	4½	0 3	250	9	
Jam ..	Locally r	ationed				
Fats ..	100	3½				Including 50 grammes butter in certain areas

Meat :
  Urban
    areas
	180	6½				

Rural areas	125	4½				
Fish ⎫ Poultry ⎬	Locally r	ationed				
Cheese ..	50	2				
Fruit and ⎫ vegetables ⎭	Locally r	ationed				
Chocolate	no	ne	0–6	30	1	
			6–20	60	2	
Coffee (mixed with substitute)	35	1¼	None for chil	dren 0–6		
or Chicory ..	45	1½				

FRANCE—*Continued*

	Normal Consumer		Children and Young People			Notes
			age	litres	pints	3·5 litres or 6
Milk (whole)	no	ne	0–6	5·25	9	pints to expectant
			6–14	1·75	3	and nursing
Milk (skimmed)	Unration	ed but availa	not ble	always		mothers
				grammes	lb. oz.	
Babies' foods	no	ne	0–6	60	2	

GREECE

No ration tables available

LUXEMBURG (May 1942)

	Normal Consumer		Children and Young People			Notes
	grammes	lb. oz.	age	gms.	lb. oz.	
Bread ..	2,000	4 6	0–3	900	2 0	
			3–6	1,200	2 10	
			6–10	1,700	3 12	
			10–20	2,600	5 12	
Flour ⎫ Cakes ⎬ Pastries ⎭	On specified bread coupons					
Processed cereals	130	4½	0–3	275	9½	
			3–6	212	7½	
Potatoes..	2,500	5½				
Sugar ..	225	8				
Jam ..	175	6	6–14	225	8	
Artificial honey	none		0–10	31	1	
Fats ..	203	7	0–3	125	4½	
			3–6	188	6½	
			6–10	256	9½	
			10–20	269	9½	
Meat ..	300	10½	0–6	150	5½	
			6–10	350	12½	
Cheese ..	47	1½				
Quark* ..	30	1				
Eggs (per 2 weeks)	one					
Cocoa ..	none		0–10	15	½	
Coffee substitute	78	2½	0–3	none		
				litres	pints	
Milk (whole)	none		0–3	5·25	9	3·5 litres or 6
			3–6	3·5	6	pints for
			6–10	1·75	3	nursing mothers

*Whey-cheese

THE NETHERLANDS (June 1942)

	Normal Consumer		Children and Young People				Notes
	grammes	lb. oz.	age	grms.	lb.	oz.	
Bread ..	1,800	3 15	0–4	900	2		Households
			4–14	1,800	3	15	with a yearly
			14–20	2,200	4	15	income below
							1,400 guilders.
							500 grammes
							more per
							week
Biscuits ⎫ Cakes ⎬ Pastries ⎭	on bread	coupons					
Flour ..	70	2½					
Cereal products and alimentary pastes ..	88	3					
Rice ..	none		0–4	125		4½	
Potatoes..	2,500	5 10	0–4	1,250	2	13	Not always
			4–14	2,500	5	10	available
			14–20	3,750	8	7	
Pulses ..	188	6½					
Sugar ..	250	9					
Jam ..	125	4½					
Butter ..	175	6	0–4	75		2½	
Meat (without bones)	175	6	0–4	87		3	
			4–20	175		6	
Eggs ..	none						
Cheese (skimmed milk)	125	4½	0–20	125		4½	
Cocoa ..	none						
Coffee substitute	63	2					
	litres	pints		litres	pints		
Milk (whole)	none		0–4	5·25	9		
			4–14	3·5	6		
Milk (skimmed)	2·1	3¾	0–14	none			Estimate as
			14–20	2·1	3¾		rationed by
							retailers

NORWAY (May 1942)

	Normal Consumer		Children and Young People			Notes
	grammes	lb. oz.	age	grms.	lb. oz.	
Bread ..	1,820	4 1	0–6	910	2	
or						
Flour ..	1,400	3 2	0–6	700	1 9	
or						
Hard bread	1,120	2 8	0–6	560	1 4	
Rice ..	25	1				
Potatoes..	Locally rationed, generally 250 to 750 grammes, i.e. 9 oz. to 1 lb. and 11 oz., but not always fully available					
Sugar ..	200	7				
Syrup ..	135	5				
Fats ..	210	7½				
Meat ..	100	3½				
Chocolate	none		2 13	37	1¼	
Coffee substitute	50	2	0–6		none	
	litres	pints	litres		pints	
Milk (whole)	none		0–5	5·25	9	7 litres i.e. 12 pints for pregnant women
			5–16	3·5	6	
			16–18	1·75	3	
Milk (skimmed)	1·75	3				If available

Note.—Non-rationed commodities very rare or available to producers only, like eggs and cheese.

POLAND (Warsaw, October–December 1941)

	Consumer		Children 2 to 12		Notes
	grammes	lb. oz.	grammes	lb. oz.	
Rye Bread .	1,525	3 6	1,220	2 11½	Children under
Wheat flour	66·6	2	143	5	2 are not en-
Biscuits ..	no	ne	50	1½	titled to ration
					cards
Potatoes ..	60 kilogr	ammes (	1 cwt. and	22¼ lb.)	Full rations
	per	family f	or the win	ter	practically
					never available
Sugar ..	108	4			
Jam ..	87	3			
Melted					
butter ..	17	½			
Meat					
(including					
bones)	150	5			Per ten days
Eggs ..	1				
Candies ..	33	1	63	2	
Coffee					
substitute	19	½			
Milk			age grms.		Not fully avail-
(whole)	no	ne	0–1 3·5	6	able.
(skimmed)	no	ne	1–2 3·5	6	On medical cer-
			2–12 3·5	6	tificate only.

POLAND (Incorporated Area. Summer 1941)

	Germans (minimum)		Poles (maximum)		Notes
	grammes	lb. oz.	grammes	lb. oz.	
Rye bread .			1,750	3 14	The flour can
Rye flour ..			375	13	be replaced by 500 grammes bread Children under 2, 400 grammes (140 oz. of bread)
Gruel, rice *or* macaroni	300	10½	100–225	3½–8	Gruel only for Poles & not always available
Artificial honey ..	250	9	100–175	3½–6	
Jam ..	unrestricted				
Butter *or* margarine	250	9	100	3½	Butter exceptional for Poles 75 grammes (2½ oz. for children under 2
Meat ..	750	1 11	250	9	Beef only for Poles and 100 grammes for children under 2
Cheese ..	unrestricted		forbidden		
Cream cheese ..	,,		25	1	
	litres	pints	litres	pints	
Milk :					
Adults :	none		none		
Children 0–2 :	7	12	3·5	6	Only if available
,, 2–12 :	3·5	6	none		

YUGOSLAVIA (June 1942)

	Normal Consumer				
	SERBIA		CROATIA		
	grammes	lb. oz.	grammes	lb. oz.	
Bread ..	1,400	3 1	1,050	2 5½	
Sugar ..	140	5	116	4	
Butter ..	none		23	1	
Cooking fat ..	95	3	116	4	
Meat	300	10½	500	1 2	

FINLAND (May 1942)

	Normal Consumer		Children				Notes
	grammes	lb. oz.	age	grms.	lb. oz.		
Bread ..	1,750	3 14	0–3	1,050	2 5		
			4–7	1,400	3 1		
Cereal products	85	3	0–7	230	8		
Potatoes..	Locally rationed						
Potato flour	12	⅓					
Pulses ..	60	2					
Sugar ..	250	9					
Syrup, jam or fruit juice	125	4½					
Fats (including cheese)	62	2	0–7	120	4		
Meat ..	150	5½					
Fish ..	Locally rationed						
Dried fruit	10	⅓					One coupon for 250 grammes (9 oz.) in six months
	litres	pints		litres	pints		
Milk ..	1·4	2½	0–6	5·25	9		3·5 litres or 6 pints for nursing mothers
			6–14	3·5	6		

COMPARATIVE TABLE OF WEEKLY RATIONS

NORMAL CONSUMER ONLY—FIRST HALF OF 1942

Commodities	Great Britain	Belgium	Czecho-slovakia	Denmark	France	Greece	Luxem-burg	Nether-lands	Norway	Poland (Gov. Gen.) 1941	Yugo-slavia (Serbia)	Finland
	Oz.	Oz.	Oz.	Oz.	Oz.	Oz.	Oz.	Oz.	Oz.	Oz.	Oz.	Oz.
Bread	U.	55 on bread coupns	72 on bread coupns	80	68 on bread coupns	51 on bread coupns	70 on bread coupns	63	55 on bread coupns	54*	49	62¹¹⁰⁄₃
Flour								2½ on b.c.		2*		
Biscuits	Points									0		3
Cereals	Points				on bread coupns			3				
Groats	U.	2½	1½	9⁴								
Oatmeal	U.						4½					L.
Potatoes		123*	88	U.	L.16–72²		88	90	L.9–27	1¼ cwt. per family for the winter		
Macaroni	U.				2²			3 instead of cereals				
Rice	Points				6	S.					S.	
Pulses	Points	2	2		2			6½			5	2
Sugar	8	8	8	17½	4½	S.	8	9	7	4*	5	9
Jam	4	4	12½		L.		6	4½	5	3*		
Honey			6									4½
Artificial honey or syrup	Points	2½									0	
Butter	2							6				
Margarine	4	3½	6	11	3½				7½	½	3	2⁹
Lard and cooking fat	2											
Oil	U.						7					

Not available or included in the meat ration

	C1	C2	C3	C4	C5	C6	C7	C8	C9	C10	C11	C12
	5½	10½	5*[1]	3½	6	10½		4½–6½	U.*[5]	10½	6*[1]	4
Bacon	L.		O.	S.	S.		S.		U.		S.	
Meat							S.	L. L.				†
Fish			1*					L.				U.
Poultry												U.
Eggs					4½	½–2½		2				½–1
Cheese								2	O.	1	1	4
Coffee												U.
Coffee substitute			½	2	2	2½		1½				U.
Chicory										3½		
Tea	⅛								O.			2
Cocoa					O.	3			O.			U.
Chocolate									O.			}
Sweets												3
Dried fruit	S.	U.		U.	U.	U.	U.	S.				Points U.
Fresh fruit	S.	U.		U.	U.	U.	U.	L.				U.
Fresh vegetables								L.				Points
Tinned foods												Points

Generally not available

	Pints	Pints	Pints	Pints	Pints	Pints	Pints	Pints	Pints	Pints	Pints	Pints
Whole milk, normal consumer / Children	2½; 0–6:9, 6–14:3		O.; 0–1:6*	O.; 0–5:9, 5–16:5, 16–18:3	O.; 0–5:9, 4–14:6	O.; 0–3:9, 3–6:6, 6–10:3	S. S.	O.; 0–6:9, 6–14:3	U. U.	3; 0–6:6	O.; 0–3:9½, 3–6:6, 6–14:3 — L.	2³; 0–6:7, 6–17:3½, 6–14:17
Skimmed milk			O.; 1–2:6, 2–13:6⁸	3*	3¾		Not available or on milk coupons	U.*			L.	
Tinned milk			O.									Points U.
Babies' food			O.					0–5:2oz.				U.

* Supply generally insufficient and/or irregular. † 1s. 0d. worth. O. = Not available. S. = Very scarce. U. = Unrationed. L. = Rationed locally.

[1]Bones included. [2]Winter only. None in summer. U. in summer. [3]Winter only. [4]Breakfast oats or barley flour. [5]One ... meatless day a week. [6]Small rations for children only. [7]Sale restricted. [8]On medical certificate only. [9]Including cheese. [10]Potato flour

CORRIGENDUM

For "General Government" in POLAND, pages 85 to 108, *passim*, read "Government General".

The Homes for Little Boys

FARNINGHAM AND SWANLEY, KENT

Maintain nearly 400 Homeless Boys, most of them fatherless, many of them motherless as well

They enter The Homes as little boys, some of them tiny toddlers, just able to walk. They leave The Homes as young men, competent to earn their own living.

No friendless boy leaves Farningham until he has served a complete apprenticeship in the trade of his choice, and has had a situation found for him, or entrance direct into the Navy, Army or Air Force, in the Service of King and Country.

For over 70 Years old friends of The Homes have generously made possible this noble work, which costs over **£25,000** a year. But during recent years death has removed so many old friends that new friends are needed if the good work is to continue.

NO GIFT IS TOO SMALL TO BE GRATEFULLY ACKNOWLEDGED.

Royal Patrons : **H.M. THE KING and H.M. QUEEN MARY.** President : W. LINTS SMITH, Esq. ; Hon. Treasurer : Col. A. E. MARNHAM, M.C., T.D., D.L. ; Chairman : DAVID H. LINDSAY, Esq. ; Secretary : JOHN ARTHUR BELL.

SAVING THE NATION'S CHILDREN

Evacuation schemes have revealed to a wider public the wretched conditions in which thousands of children have to live. To the National Children's Home the position was only too well known. For over 73 years it has been saving boys and girls from these conditions and giving them the chance every child should have as a right. While such blots on our social life remain, the work of the Home must go on. But the war has made things difficult and funds are urgently needed. We appeal for your special help in a time of urgent necessity.

NATIONAL CHILDREN'S HOME

Chief Offices: HIGHBURY PARK, LONDON, N.5.   *(Founded by Dr. Stephenson 1869)*   AND ORPHANAGE

POST WAR PRINTING

THE launching of schemes for the benefit of mankind and the reconstruction of the world when peace has been restored will need the services of the Printing Presses up and down the country. We hope to be in a position to offer Lay-outs—selection of modern Type Faces—and advice on all matters appertaining to the printed word—so essential to the author.

REMEMBER

THE

London Caledonian Press Ltd.

74 SWINTON STREET, LONDON, W.C.1

Telephone : TERminus *6601